THE CORRUPTION OF A POET

By KENNETH HOPKINS

LOVE AND ELIZABETH
MISCELLANY POEMS
SONGS AND SONNETS
POEMS ON SEVERAL OCCASIONS
TO A GREEN LIZARD
APES AND ELDERBERRIES

THE ENGLISH LYRIC

EDMUND BLUNDEN:
a selection from his writings

LLEWELYN POWYS:
a selection from his writings

H. M. TOMLINSON:
a selection from his writings

WALTER DE LA MARE

THE POETS LAUREATE

St. John and the Author

KENNETH HOPKINS

THE CORRUPTION
OF A POET

The corruption of a poet is
the generation of a critic.

JOHN DRYDEN

LONDON
JAMES BARRIE
1954

First published 1954

MADE IN GREAT BRITAIN
Printed by
The Garden City Press, Limited
Letchworth, Herts.

*To my Mother and
in memory of
my Father*

Acknowledgements

The author thanks The Sylvan Press for permission to quote poems from *Love and Elizabeth*, and the Editors of *Enquiry*, the *Evening Standard*, *The Folio*, the *Literary Digest*, *John o' London's Weekly*, *The Spectator*, and *Time and Tide*, in which some passages of this book have appeared.

Contents

If thou hast any excellence which is thine own thy tongue may glory in it without shame.

Francis Quarles

Forgotten Summers

Like most of us, I have frequently had an inner prompting to write my autobiography. This prompting I have steadfastly ignored and, as I am now at an age (thirty-nine) when many people have written their autobiography at least once, I feel that I owe it to myself to explain my tardiness.

Looking back at my life I can see that it is (although comparatively commonplace) one that might well be recorded under some such title as *Winter of Discontent* or *Prejudice in Paradise*—and indeed even thus early in the enterprise I am tempted to earmark the second; but we'll see.

Yet—I ask myself (for doubt early sets in)—is it enough to have been successively a baby, a schoolboy, the idle apprentice of an ironmonger, a commercial traveller in various sorts of merchandise, a confirmed dole-drawer, a dustman, a lance-corporal, and finally what I am today?

In all these necessary human activities I have been at best but one of a crowd—at one time, for example, there were more lance-corporals in our mob than privates. Again, the man who publishes his autobiography must either have seen extraordinary days, or must write extraordinarily well. Alas . . .

I will come straight to the point. The real reason why I cannot write my autobiography is that *I cannot remember any of the summers I have seen.* Now, I have noticed that all successful autobiographies (and I would not attempt any other sort) contain a series of chapters under such titles as "I am Born", "Eton in the 'Eighties" and probably, in reference to some great house, "Childhood at Slopley".

I could do all that—the happy times at 41, Southcote Road, where my mother took up residence during father's absence at the war. (A short chapter, I think, for there were no grounds except a two-yard square of privet hedge, and the premises themselves were no Chatsworth. We had two rooms, commanding extensive views of 26, Southcote Road, just opposite.) I could also do the Lulworth Villa Schools kept by the Misses Alexander. On my way there, on my first day, I lost my lunch. It was there, too, that I won my first prize, a book called *Mother's Warm Shawl*, which I think had similarly been won fifty years earlier by Miss Emily Alexander. It was decidedly old-fashioned reading.

I could even do the preliminary stuff about my ancestors, the great-grandfather who looked like A. Trollope but was a house-painter, and other worthies whose combined efforts and influence resulted in my appearance on December 7, 1914.

But, *what about the summers?*

The autobiographer who is my ideal, and my model, is almost certain to discuss the glory of Sussex in '07 and a last wicket stand of twelve which vitally affected the averages. Then he will recall long expeditions to Waldegrave Spinney in search of an alleged colony of Camberwell Beauties. Once, sailing his boat in the July sunshine on the Round Pond he was patted on the head by Holman Hunt. It was in summer, too, in the drowsy heat of the great marquee at the Vicarage Fete, that he first kissed Rose Wilkins, aged thirteen.

But I never caught so much as a Cabbage White and my inability to play or even to understand cricket is largely responsible for the disappointed expression I wear today. I was also unlucky in love, probably because I used to wear a shiny black mackintosh and a wolf cub cap.

Now I am good at winters. The winters in our parts were usually chilly and wet and my shiny black mackintosh came in handy. I was only eleven when I won a pair of military hairbrushes at a whist drive. Another thing about the winters was that they had my birthday in them. When I was four somebody gave me a drum and I beat it with a fork, I think to most people's secret relief, for after one shrewd blow it wouldn't yield a note and in the end we made it into two hoops. My birthday also occurred in winter the year I was six, and I remember asking my cousin Winnie almost before she got in the door and took her coat off, where my present was. It turned out to be a blackboard and a piece of chalk, which was, I suppose, the repository of my first writings. They have not survived, and the blackboard itself was a casualty of the hard winter of '26, the time we had no coal.

In winter I would go home from choir practice reading *Nelson Lee* by the light of an electric torch. That's how I got this scar over my left eye. With the same torch I used to creep down to the bottom of the bed, under the bedclothes and read *Fifteen Decisive Battles of the World*, except "Victory of the Americans over Burgoyne at Saratoga, A.D. 1777," which I thought it rather unpatriotic of Sir Edward Creasy to have recorded. After all, he could have made a decent-size book with only fourteen battles. However, so far as I could tell, we won most of the others.

I am also quite good with autumn. That was conker time. I was very clever at collecting conkers, but quite unable to control them in combat. I never owned a "hundred-and-one-er", but I have had many likely nuts beaten to pulp before my anguished eyes. I think, though, that many little boys cheat, a thing I never had the wit to do. On one occasion I remember an opponent who had announced before the battle that his was a sixer or a nineteener, or whatever it was, afterwards going into his next contest with a twenty-eighter—or whatever it was. He based this great advance on the fact that with his last blow he had carried away my conker, the string, and the end of my finger. In the same spirit, a small child called Ronnie with whom I played a kind of cricket once in Spencer Gardens claimed to have made a century not out. This he had achieved in two ways: first by not letting me bat anyway, because it was his bat; and next, by counting it as a run to himself when I ran after the ball, so that his rate of scoring was approximately double the normal. It was also his ball, and I counted myself lucky in being allowed to play; but the experience confirmed me in my comparative lack of interest in cricket.

I was fond of going different ways to school and counting the number of paces. Littledown Road, I can tell you, is nine hundred paces from the top of the railway steps to the junction with Trinity Road. I suppose it would have been the same in summer; but somehow pace-counting seems essentially an occupation for October.

I think I could fill a few pages with spring memories— certainly enough to get by. It was spring, thirteen years ago, when I joined the army. The town of Derby in spring is just the place to join the army in; but—six weeks' basic training over— what of Derby in high summer? I can recall nothing.

What was I doing in the summer of '24, when the Wembley Exhibition was in full swing? Where was I in the summer of '21, when all the rivers dried up? In '29, '30, and the rest? I cannot tell.

I have forgotten all my summers, no doubt because we were never taken to the seaside. We already lived there. Thus, the most exciting of August activities never came my way. I have never owned a bucket and spade, and now I am old enough to buy one for myself I live at Brighton where there is no sand.

We had no garden, no glebe or paddock or Home Farm or kitchen garden, and certainly no gardener, no stable boy. As a matter of fact, my father kept his bicycle under an old ground-sheet. He was one of the last of the generation that got on a bike by shuffling along behind it and climbing up over the back step. I never saw him fall off, but it is not a method I ever favoured myself. When you are shuffling along in that way the front end of the bike is almost out of sight, the steering is erratic, and a toe not firmly and accurately placed on the back-step is apt to get into the spokes.

Cricket, no. Seaside, no. Long birds-nesting expeditions to Waldegrave Spinney, no. Not even a birthday to be looked forward to. No wonder the dusty summer months were a desert to me as I kicked a tennis ball along the interminable gutters. The only time I ever fell in love was at a Christmas Party, and when I'd got all dressed and muffled up to take her home, I remembered that she lived next door.

As, therefore, I again approach my autobiography, I am once more confronted by this teasing difficulty. I have spoken of it in a guarded way to a number of eminent autobiographers. I usually begin with a cautious reference to the weather of '28. "A hard winter that was," I say, and no one has ever denied it. "The summer of '29, now . . ." I continue wistfully, pausing with a civil leer to give them time to speak.

"Have you read Polwhele's *Lucretius*?" they answer.

The beginning of my autobiography, the first two chapters, I can do any time: Chapter One, "Ancestry", and Chapter Two, "Birth at Bournemouth". These chapters take my life story up to the end of May, 1915, when I was six months old and—let's admit it—they are comparatively uneventful. Something more will be needed.

I am convinced that if I could recall those errant summers I have the makings of an autobiographer of the highest class. One gentleman whose *Memoirs of his own Time* was a *must* on every library list has whispered the only alternative to me behind his hand on the top of a 16 bus:

"Make it up!" he said. "It's your word against theirs."

Ancestry

There is a photograph of my father marching to the wars in 1914, a couple of months before I was born. He was in the 5/7th Hants., and some part of that gallant regiment, including my father (fifth in eighth row from left), is seen splendidly proceeding over the railway bridge in Holdenhurst Road in the direction of the Lansdowne. At one time I used to think that they took ship somewhere down by the pier and thus were whisked away, but I think they probably took a right turn into the station yard because they were going, in fact, to Salisbury Plain.

I never took a great interest in my ancestry, perhaps because we had no Long Gallery, as they had at Slopley, with generations of former Earls looking haughtily out of their painted canvases like connoisseurs about to recommend a brand of whisky. The only ancestral portrait I have is great-grandfather Hopkins, the one who looked like A. Trollope. He really does look like him; and of course they were contemporaries; Trollope, I think, would have been interested to know that they preserve at Bournemouth as a curiosity the pillar-box in which Mr. Gladstone used to post letters when staying in the town. The preservation of this is in no way connected with great-grandfather, but as a house-painter perhaps he sometimes had occasion to renovate the receptacle, though even this is doubtful, for great-grandfather was no ordinary painter. He was, properly, a grainer, and in those days graining was an art. Great-grandfather could grain whitewood to look like the rarest and most elaborate hardwoods, the birdseyes and the rest. They do say that much of the graining he did when the Royal Bath Hotel was first built is still there, under some forty coats of varnish, as black now as any Old Master, but still indubitably birdseye or whatever. Great-grandfather was the man who kept the hotel being built longer than they expected because none-but-he could do the graining, and some of the time the daily grind with him went against the grain and he took a few days rest.

His tinted photograph in a heavy gilt frame is, as I have admitted, the only family portrait of any antiquity I have. There is a curious story concerning this portrait and before I set it down I want to say, quite soberly, that it is perfectly true.

When we lived in Cambridge Gardens, off Ladbroke Grove, great-grandfather for reasons beyond our control had to be accommodated in the attic; he was not forgotten, and he hung in quite a good light and was passed by everyone on the way to the bathroom. He hung over the fireplace.

One day when we returned home (the flat having been locked and empty) we found great-grandfather face downwards half in the room and half on the landing, about five or six feet from where he had been hanging. The string on the frame was not broken, and neither was the frame or its glass. The nail upon which it had been hanging was safe and secure in the wall.

I reckon great-grandfather had been on his way to grain the wardrobe in the spare bedroom.

There were other odd things about that flat. Quite often the electric light in great-grandfather's room would be on when we came in although it had been off when we went out. Also, Betty often heard me come in from the office at night when, in fact, I had done nothing of the kind. Then there was once a loud crash from great-grandfather's quarters, which were directly above our bedroom. But nothing there was found to be displaced. I mention these things, not to get great-grandfather into trouble, but because they have never been explained, and now that we don't live there any more I suppose they never will be. I am ashamed to say that at present, on account that

2

we have no attics, great-grandfather is standing with his face to
the wall in Anne's room (which is so named, but has no
occupant.) But he will come into his own again, for they say
that tinted photographs, circa. 1860, are becoming quite
fashionable.

We have, I believe, no residences in our family going back
more than half a century; I know of only two which might be
called ancestral. On the edge of Pug's Hole, in Talbot Woods,
there was once pointed out to me a cottage in which some
ancient relative was said to be living; and in Ship House Lane,
Iford-way, I was once shown a cottage with mud walls connected in some obscure fashion with the family name. Mud as
a building material has, I suppose, gone right out. It made a
sound wall, properly used, and took the best of birdseye
graining to perfection.

In the chapel graveyard at Throop there are some family
graves; these, too, were once pointed out to me, and there
are others, I believe, in the churchyard at Holdenhurst.
But I confess I am a little hazy about it all; most of these items
of ancient family history were imparted to me when I was, I
think, seven. It seemed then a long time ago, and it now seems
even longer.

I hope it will not be thought that great-grandfather Hopkins is
the only ancestor I have. Not a bit of it. I am assured there was
great-grandmother, too; but of this lady I confess I have learned
nothing, and even grandfather and grandmother Hopkins
were before my time. Wait! I once went to visit grandmother
Hopkins at Cole Hill—was it? Another of those expeditions at
the age of seven which in these after-years are the foundation of
my knowledge of family history.

My mother's parents I never knew, but I know we went down
to Yeovil once to stay, and from thence went to visit Montacute,
where my mother had lived as a girl. I have also heard rumours
of a sub-Post Office in those parts with which there are distant
family connections though nothing, I think, to justify the
reintroduction of Trollope. Trollope, by the way, is not alone

in his connection with the Post Office; there's all about it in the autobiography of Edmund Yates, whose novels were well thought of in the days of my great-grandfather.

My sister and I once worked out that we had sixty cousins; a cousin, after all, is a fairly close sort of relation. They ought all to buy this book.

Birth at Bournemouth

I was born at Bournemouth on December 7, 1914. Of this I have no doubt, for at various times I have had three birth certificates to prove it. The first was when I got married, the next was when I joined the army, and the third was to support my application for a passport. The fact that in all these enterprises I was successful also tends to confirm the statement.

Oh, I was born all right! The house is still pointed out to the curious (who cannot be more curious than the house is: it is one storey high, about sixteen feet wide at the front, and tapers off to a point at the back.) This establishment is number 133, Southcote Road, Bournemouth. If ever you see a book called *From Isosceles Triangle to White House*, you will know I have become President of the United States.

I have never discovered why I was born at 133 when we lived at 41; especially as at 49 there was another branch of the family commanded by Aunt Ada. But I expect the explanation is perfectly simple.

At 41—Mrs. Clarke's—we had the downstairs front room as a bed-sitting room. At 133, which was a lock-up shop, we had the back-room to live in and behind that, in the extreme tip of the point the premises ran off to, there was a lavatory and wash-basin. Behind this was a bit of garden, running off to another point; and beyond, the Generating Station and tram sheds.

Behind 41 was a steel-joist works; and behind Aunt Ada's a bit of garden with chickens and then a stock-yard for chimney pots and slates and drain pipes, owned then by Sharp, Jones. I used to think this was a clever gentleman and not a limited company.

Walter de la Mare once asked me what was the first thing I could remember, and off and on ever since that day I have puzzled at the same question. I don't know the answer. The *first* thing? It ought to be something before I could walk, I suppose: some memory of being carried here or there, perhaps, or of being lifted up. They tell me I could walk at ten months, so such a recollection would indeed go back a long way. The easier thing, I suppose, would be to fix what was going on and then see if one remembered it. On December 8, 1914, was fought the Battle of the Falkland Islands; my uncle Perce was there in one of the cruisers. I was one day old and unaware of these things being done on that far side of the world. Battle of Jutland, 1916; I was rising two. Again no recollection.

But some things I recall from the war years, so I suppose they must be my earliest memories. Sitting on the beach and watching airships—"pigs", my mother used to call them, and I always later associated them with the expression, pigs may fly. I hope those airships were on our side, because we used to go on sitting there. On another occasion unknown to myself I had made a deep scratch in my leg, probably on a piece of glass or sharp stone in the sand. "Look, he's wounded!" remarked a soldier who was taking a rest from battle by talking to Aunt Ada. How we all scurried to the ambulance tent which in those days stood on the grass just inside Bournemouth Gardens, opposite the pier entrance.

My mother says that in those years she used to keep as still as a mouse in the back room of 133 and pray that my sister and I would not squeak while the soldiers went by late at night on their way back to billets. Apparently they were fond of our little back garden for various nocturnal pieces of business. One day—says my mother—when she had unaccountably omitted to bolt, bar and lock the front door it flew open with a crash and a soldier and his girl who had been leaning against it descended into the shop. I have never discovered if they passed the thing off by attempting to make a purchase; and as this is not my mother's autobiography I had better return to matters that come directly within my own recollection, like the time when my sister broke one of her teeth.

This happened in a large crust of bread and jam which she was eating in the garden and resulted in a very small stain of blood appearing on the end of the crust. So we both had to have completely new crusts of bread and jam handed out through the lavatory window, which was done to save the journey round to the front—for 133 had no back door: and indeed there would have been no room for a back door. I can only hope they were the same crusts trimmed a bit; I expect they were. This mention of jam reminds me of the marmalade we used to have in cardboard pots, tasting right at the end increasingly of cardboard. That was in the days of rationing, which otherwise I can't recall. We never went without our cake on Sunday morning—my sister and I had half each with the morning tea. These cakes were those round spongy ones with cream in the middle and two wing-like pieces sticking up on top. Old Mr. Clarke used to bring a pot of tea every Sunday morning and leave it at the bed-sitting-room door—back at 41, now; it is really most confusing, but I must tell the story the way I remember it.

Mr. Clarke was a phrenologist. For many years he had a shop in Boscombe Arcade and predicted great things for me after a careful exploration of the bumps on my head (one or two of which might have been mere ephemera, I fear, caused by table legs and other natural hazards.) Still, who is to say he wasn't right—it may turn out in the end that I really have the formidable genius he claimed to have detected. If I haven't, it won't be for want of hoping.

It was Mr. Clarke whom I first saw using a razor; the sight gave me great satisfaction, but I couldn't see why soap needed to be scraped off when it comes away very readily on a flannel. So far as I could tell, this peculiar practice was confined to Mr. Clarke alone in the whole household, and by him was employed only on his face. This mystery, however, was but one of the many I encountered in those early years, some of which I have not yet satisfactorily cleared up.

My father had gone to the wars before I was born, and as his regiment served in India he remained invisible for five years. In this time my idea of what a father was remained distinctly hazy; but I kept in touch with him by insisting on enclosing an ivy-leaf in the letters my mother wrote. There was one spot in Boscombe Gardens where the ivy leaves were uncommonly large, and it was usually one of these that I chose. I could go to the identical place today and as ivy still grows there I might even find some leaves—now grown no doubt to gigantic proportions—which then escaped my researches. For ivy is an evergreen.

On the same path a year or two later I picked up a brown paper parcel, which I proceeded to take from one passer-by to another without identifying anyone who had dropped it. In the end I took it home and found it contained two pairs of socks; I mention this trifling acquisition because generally speaking in all my life I have had very little luck in the way of recovering lost treasure. The odd penny or sixpence, now and then, and once a half-crown wedged upright between two rocks at low tide at Studland; but otherwise nothing but these two pairs of socks; and of course they wore out long since. It must be all of thirty years ago. I suppose this chapter ought to finish soon; I have explained when and where I was born and brought myself more or less to the age of four.

One thing I clearly remember is my father coming home from the war. We all went up to the station to meet him—my mother, my sister, me, and all Aunt Ada's lot: we made quite a little army ourselves.

About the time the train was due I had to be taken home to go to the lavatory.

And we met them all coming back in triumph with my father in the middle dressed as a soldier. So far as I recall, I hadn't expected him to look like that.

The Misses Alexander

I don't know how these young fellows manage who write their autobiographies at the age of twenty or so; here I am already past the age of five, the war over and everything, and only on page twenty-four. I see I have dismissed the Battle of Jutland in a sentence: true, I wasn't there, but even so it ought to have been good for a paragraph. No doubt my early training in short story writing is having this effect. I must try not to hurry so quickly over my schooldays.

I was sent first to the Lulworth Villa Schools (The Misses Alexander). My sister was already attending this select academy and doing well. As for my brother—do you know, I didn't even know I had one! The thing was a complete surprise to me.

A few weeks after my father came back from the war I asked my mother how much longer that man was going to stay with us: for good! she told me. Now, another chap was coming, I learned. This was brother Douglas—in strict fact, my half brother, who had been living at Rochester during the war years. Douglas had all sorts of exciting belongings, including Meccano and one of those little steam engines that turn a wheel. Remarkable! But as Douglas never came to the Misses Alexander perhaps I am going too fast in my anxiety to get to the steam engine. Let it lie at Rochester a little longer.

Miss Alexander was almost too grand for me to speak to, and I was taught by Miss Emily in the back room. Was it the Lulworth Villas School, or the Lulworth Villa Schools?—I can never be sure. Anyway, Lulworth Villa(s) was a small semi-detached house with (I suppose) six rooms. It had a front door which was never opened, not for mere scholars, anyway, and a back door which led through the kitchen into Miss Emily's

classroom by way of a little narrow lobby or passage. The
front room was Miss Alexander's classroom. These ancient
ladies if they are still alive will now be about a hundred and
thirty; and doubtless still wearing little bands of velvet round
the middle of their throats like dog collars.

One astonishing feature of the drive up to the front door
(which was set back perhaps twenty feet from the road,
perhaps only fifteen) was a pine tree which shot up through
the middle of the gravel path—which was only about thirty
inches wide, anyway. So one had to pass either to the left or to
the right of this "very reverend vegetable" (I borrow the phrase
from Thomas Gray, who first applied it to William Mason
I dare say) and the odd thing is, I always passed to the left
going and to the right coming back.

The school(s) had quite a big playground, running down to
the backs of the cottages in Annerley Road. Just outside the
back door there was a patch of kitchen garden, a gooseberry
bush or two and so on; you went down a little path and then
there was the playground. What we played I cannot tell, for I
have forgotten, but it was here, I think, that Bobby gave me
the pencil box for my birthday which shut on my fingers.

I suppose I ought to say something about my contemporaries.
This Bobby, for example, for about three years was my best
friend. More than that, I know nothing about him.

Nathan I remember more clearly. He wore knickerbockers,
and long black stockings which I thought uncommonly
dashing. He used to smell of weak tea. After one term he
didn't come any more.

The other little boy I remember was Kenneth Callow who
used to explain earnestly to anyone that would listen that his
real name was Kale. It would be useless to question me further
upon this matter, although I have puzzled over it off and on for
thirty years. That was his story; it never varied, and he never
added to it. "They call me Kenneth Callow, but my real name
is Kenneth Kale." In my experience there is only one parallel,
and that is not a very close one. At St. Peter's School, later, we

had for a while a lad whose name was Schragal and everyone called him Shredgold; "Never mind, Schragal," Wiggy Bennett would say; and to give the lad his due, I believe he never did mind. He was another one who only stayed a term.

There were little girls at the Misses Alexander's school but apart from my sister I can't remember any of them.

What did we learn? Good manners, certainly (as anybody who knows me today will tell you, sometimes with tears in their eyes.) Geography, I think, and History, I know, because it was History that brought me up against one of life's realities. On our birthday we used to be allowed to choose which book we would be read to out of (the phrase is not mine, but custom hallows it). I chose a book called "Modern English History" and Miss Emily said wouldn't it be much nicer, because modern history was very dull, if we had the Wars of the Roses. What sort of a birthday treat was that? I have been resentful about the whole thing ever since, and ever on the lookout for a book called "Modern English History".[1] I dare say by the time I come across it, the contents will be as ancient as the rest of history. Anyway, it opened my eyes to the fact that history is going on all the time, which was something the others didn't suspect.

The only other thing—two things—I remember about that school—no three! how it all comes back!

At the end of term everybody got a prize, sometimes on the flimsiest pretext (like the policeman in Belloc's novel, who got promoted for not having done anything silly). On the big round table in Miss Alexander's room were spread two or three dozen books, and we were allowed to choose one each. I turned them over, even in those days, with the eager nonchalance of the bibliophile. The work I chose—*Mother's Warm Shawl*—I have already referred to briefly. If it was a first edition, it would be quite valuable today, no doubt, if I still had it. But I have

[1] It was not, of course, W. J. Cory's *Modern English History* (1880–82), that rare and excellent book.

no books surviving from those far off days. Even my copy of
Fifteen Decisive Battles is not the same, although it is the same
edition in that attractive red cloth.

The next thing I remember is that after the summer holidays
the Misses Alexander brought each of us back from Swanage, or
wherever it was that they went, an ear of ripe corn, and showed
us how to get out the little nut-like kernels and eat them. I
didn't think much of the stuff myself. Goodness, though, what
a mess we made on the floor—and corn husks take a bit of
sweeping off carpets.

Finally, before leaving the Lulworth Villa I must record that
one day the whole school was assembled to go out for a walk!
Such a thing was unheard of, but apparently it was to mark
half-term—or possibly the Misses Alexander couldn't face
being shut up for yet another hot summer afternoon with
twenty or thirty little children. I couldn't myself, now.

Everyone was to be allowed to participate in this treat if they
had not forfeited more than ten marks for lateness during the
term. I decided with great honesty that I had. Accordingly,
I made preparations not to go: didn't get my hat, didn't look
modestly subdued but buoyant, etc. So Miss Emily asked me if
I wasn't well, and when I said I was all right shuffled me along
with the rest.

I mention this trivial incident because it taught me a useful
lesson: that honesty is a convenience, not a fetish; and if this
taught me, something that happened a year or two later
underlined it.

Once a week we used to go to the swimming baths (I refer
now to my days at St. Peter's.) One week the master said that
if the non-swimmers didn't pull their socks up and swim at
least a few strokes this week they wouldn't go to the baths next
week. I failed to swim even half a stroke, so the following week
I turned up at school without a towel or bathing costume. My,
what a fuss they made! And I was only doing what I thought
was proper: I had not learned to swim, and non-learners to
swim were not going. So why burden oneself with a redundant

bathing costume etc.? Apparently he hadn't meant it, but how was I to know?

I recall very dimly indeed having a pram; rather more clearly, since I slept in it for about eight years, an iron cot; and quite clearly a pushchair in which I was conveyed on long expeditions. I suppose my sister walked, for I cannot recall ever giving her a lift.

How old do children go on being transported in pushchairs? Up till about six, I suppose; though I certainly did not get taken to the Lulworth Villas by this method. Our most frequent itinerary was to Wallisdown, where Aunt Eff lived; or to Winton, where lived Uncle Ham and Auntie Pris.

Aunt Eff and Uncle George, with cousins Ruby and George, lived almost in the country. There were cows just over the way and all sorts of rural refinements which Southcote Road seldom afforded (though I once met two elephants there, late at night). Aunt Eff had a number of clocks hanging on the wall with carved or painted faces; and Uncle George had a beard and drank tea out of a flowered quart pot. I used to be sent into the garden to chase the chickens, and also I was permitted to eat the gooseberries and black currants. Now and then we would be sent to stay the night at Aunt Eff's and it was on one of these occasions that I saw (probably on the top of a wardrobe) a great store of home-made jams. I returned home and reported the discovery to my mother: "Aunt Eff has thousands and thousands of pots of jam!" Here was something happening at the age of about six which influenced me thirty years later in writing a poem: an indication of how long some trivial incident will lie in wait before getting itself into print. The jam-pots are apparently only incidental in the little poem; but without them it might have remained unwritten:

THE BUBBLE

I blew myself a bubble
  That was bigger than myself
And I floated up inside it
  To the topmost shelf,

And there I saw before me
　With my own two eyes
Half a hundred jam pots
　And four dead flies.

I blew myself a bubble
　That was larger than Papa
And he floated off inside it
　To a place afar,

And everybody cheered and waved
　To see him overhead;
" Your father is a very clever man,"
　They said.

The poem also demonstrates how to a fact the writer will add a
fiction if it suits him, and let the truth go hang. My Aunt Eff
is the last person to allow dead flies to accumulate in the house.
I thought her one of the best people in the world; and I was
right.

Uncle Ham and Auntie Pris lived not quite such a long walk
away, but it seemed pretty long because a good slice of it
involved the passage of Capston Road, which I considered
nearly the longest road in the world. Unlike other roads in the
town, it had only one set of tram tracks instead of the conventional two, and I was always puzzled to know why two
trams never met somewhere in the middle going opposite ways.
Oh, they are cunning, some of these municipal departments!
They overcame that possibility by having only one tram, which
shuttled to and fro for about thirty years taking pennies. I bet
the driver came to know and heartily dislike Capston Road.
Imagine it, as straight as an arrow, disappearing interminably
into the distance, with a single set of tram tracks going mathe-
matically up the middle and this elderly tram always coming
when one desired it to be going; and vice versa.

The Winton household, and the Wallisdown one, were my
father's people. Uncle Ham had five children, Percy, Gladys,
Fred, Doris and Jack. These cousins we saw a good deal of in
those days. Then there were the four Adams cousins and Uncle

Horace and Auntie Annie, in Oxford Road; let me see, Bertha, Reenie and Doris is the right order. And Winnie the eldest who married Percy. Finally, the four cousins at 49 Southcote Road, Kitty, Maggie, Ruby and Phyllis. Also at 49 they had an extraordinary lavatory with a handle at the side which you pulled up, rather like the outside brake lever of an old-fashioned racing car. All these people were the principal characters in the first ten years or so of my existence, especially Aunt Ada's family, for after all they lived nearly next door. I was constantly in and out, sometimes without materially increasing my welcome, like when I poured a pint of paraffin into the vegetables. One of Aunt Ada's most spectacular habits was carrying the fire from room to room on a shovel, with sparks and flames and smoke streaming behind her. She was also the only woman I ever saw scrubbing the kitchen wall with a broom dipped in a bucket of soda-and-water. The chickens at 49, unlike those at Wallisdown, were frequently to be met with in the house; but this was natural enough, for they had the run of a much smaller garden. Aunt Ada also had a cloth on the mantlepiece with strings of beads hanging down the front, something I never saw anywhere else—more's the pity. When she "drew up the fire" with a newspaper she would always wait until the paper caught fire before bringing the operation to an end, and I vastly admired the dexterity with which she confined the flames within the paper by rapidly folding them up inside it until she was left with a compact and almost red hot ball. This she then placed in the grate. It was this astonishing and admirable Aunt who got me named Hector.

It was agreed from the first that I would be called Kenneth, but as my mother and Aunt Ada were walking with me to the Registry Office, Aunt Ada pointed out that the best children have two names (luckily she didn't pursue the point with those who have three, four, and so on.) What, then, else should I be called? Perhaps John, Joe and the rest were canvassed: I don't know. But I do know how the decision was reached. I was named from a Hippodrome bill which Aunt Ada noticed in which it was announced as an attraction that Hector and his Performing Fleas would be on all next week.

My early years were much influenced by various ladies. There was Aunt Sally, whom I first saw in the large kitchen of Silwood. Ah, me, how things always change for the worse! Where shall I find now such a kitchen—huge iron range, vast scrubbed dresser, row upon row of bright dinner plates? The gleaming black range had polished steel handles and knobs. All the furniture was scrubbed whitewood; the floor shone. There was always a kettle on the hob with a thread of steam drifting up from the spout—and none of your silly little tin kettles, either. This was a pot-bellied black iron kettle, holding a couple of gallons and no nonsense about it. Another thing they made proper use of in those days was the stock pot. All gone and replaced now by tin-openers, and pre-digested muck.

I suppose I was impressed by all this because at 41 and at 133 the principal cooking was done on a gas-ring. My mother had an instrument called a Dutch Oven in which she made various interesting dishes. I don't think we had a real kitchen before I was about seven so I would naturally be attracted by Auntie Sally's shining apartment.

Then there was Miss Critchley. This lady occupied a room at 41 right at the top and appeared and disappeared mysteriously night and morning. She was very small and very quiet and only really entered my consciousness after we had left and gone to live at 125. For Miss Critchley was a keen church goer and after I joined the choir was able to report that as I walked round in procession I looked like a little angel.

Nurse Kane was another small one who appeared even smaller because she lived in a basement. Every Sunday morning we used to go to her house because Auntie Rose had a bed-sitting room there, and Auntie Rose was visited as a part of the established ritual. Nurse Kane was visited any time we had a cut finger or a pain somewhere, and on those occasions Auntie Rose's room was bypassed and we proceeded straight to the basement, which was the darkest I ever saw. Mr. Kane was a schoolmaster, and I never set eyes on him, but many years afterwards, when he died, I came by his trouser press and I have used it ever since. Unfortunately when Mr. Kane acquired it trousers were cut differently from our fashion today and consequently although I can get a knife-edge crease in the lower part of my trousers I have to make a sort of fold to get the top part in. If you look closely you will see that the fine crease I have below takes a sort of right turn at the knee and goes round the back; while the back one comes round the front. All my efforts to persuade critics that this is a new fashion have failed. It is, instead, one more link in the chain of evidence which supports the view that I am eccentric.

After Mr. Kane's death I was invited to inspect his library with a view to purchase (this was when I was about fifteen, and was known to be a bit of a reader, perhaps even a scholar of a sort). He had about twenty books I discovered, of which three might have been of use to me. These were the very three Nurse Kane decided to keep—one was a copy of *Come Hither*. Another was the *Choice Works of Bret Harte*, a writer with whom I was then unacquainted. And the third was *The Wind among the Reeds*—the very copy that now stands on my shelf, though I haven't the remotest idea how it got there, nor who removed with ink-eradicator the name Kane which nonetheless can still faintly be read upon the fly-leaf. It is the third edition, an attractive book in quarter canvas, paper boards—a binding style now out of favour.

Finally I must mention Miss Towser, who lived a couple of doors away from 125. This lady used to beckon me with claw-like finger and try every persuasion to get me into her room. I with great politeness and firmness resisted. Once in, I devoted every effort to getting out again, and she would produce more and more faded photographs and boiled sweets in an attempt to detain me.

Miss Towser once gave me a small bronze figure of a god sitting cross-legged waving one fist in the air and apparently shouting imprecations. *There was a slight rattle when this figure was violently shaken.* For many years I believed a diamond or some treasure to be concealed inside, but I couldn't find the secret spring, and pen-knives had no effect upon the bronze. Finally, in 1938 I gave Scabbo (for so I called him) to my friend Boyne Grainger of New York City, and as I never heard that she had bought a yacht etc., I suppose Scabbo keeps his secret still (unless he was confiscated on entry by the Customs).

Now I must get back to the Misses Alexander, in order to leave them. They had taught me all they knew, and it was time for me to go to a real school.

Bournemouth, Beautiful and Bygone

I had better sort out these several residences. I was born at 133.
We lived during the war mainly at 41. We sometimes spent a
night or so at 49. (I mustn't complicate matters too much, but
it is as well to record that before I was born my parents lived for
a time at 65.) Soon after my father came home from the war
we bought 125, and that is still my mother's headquarters. So
the family history for forty years has been enacted in this same
Southcote Road—and always on the north side which means
houses facing south and getting the sun, but that much nearer to
the railway with its varied noises.

One-two-five was but a few doors from 133, which we retained,
and had one other attractive feature not found in the otherwise
identical 123, 127, and 129. It had a eucalyptus tree in the
front garden.

My impression is that we moved at night, taking most of our
goods in the pushchair. But I also remember sitting on top of a
lorry so perhaps we had one or two other trifles of furniture.
The lady we bought the house from had a remarkable taste in
wallpapers and her gas shades were all little bits of coloured
glass on strings which went tinkle tinkle when the doors banged,
or there was a draught.

Meanwhile my father set up his shoe repairing business again
at 133. All through the war the repairs had been collected by my
mother and passed on to Mr. Marsh, who lived in Northcote
Road, the other side of the railway. Going to Mr. Marsh was
an awfully big adventure, like dying. His little shop smelled of
shoe leather and the stains and polishes associated with
cobbling, and of rubber solution and rubber.

It was at 133 during those war years that I had my first

encounter with the great. Lady Compton-Rickett used to bring in shoes to be repaired and would sometimes pass the time of day with me. She lived in a big house on the cliffs to which we would sometimes go delivering shoes. Her husband, I have since decided, must have been Arthur Compton-Rickett the historian of English Literature and the author of various parodies and light verse. I don't think I ever met him, and I suppose we should have found hardly anything in common for I was very little advanced in his subject at four.

What an enchanting town Bournemouth was in those days! Only those who remember it in 1920 (when, the war having intervened, it was presumably virtually unchanged since 1914) can appreciate how completely it has since been spoiled. It was almost wholly Victorian and as it grew from nothing to a town of seventy thousand inhabitants in the hundred years 1810-1910 it presented a panorama of the Victorian age in architecture, planning and so on. Today it is simply a huge sprawling place with smart shops, smart hotels, smart cinemas and no individuality. I have no objection to having been born there, for we all have to be born somewhere, but I am delighted I no longer have to live there. So far as I am concerned, Bournemouth ceased to have any attractions after about 1930, when its destruction was more or less completed.

But the Bournemouth of my childhood was surely one of the most delightful towns in the country, and it was lived in by the oddest people, which of course made it all the more attractive. The East Cliff, which is now a region of large hotels, was then very secluded. Each great house stood discreetly in its own extensive grounds, presenting to the front overlooking the sea merely a remote row of shuttered windows, and to the back, in Manor Road, each its little lodge and stables. Here were the huge rhododendron plantations, the tall rows of pine trees, and the yellow brick walls behind which Privilege sheltered in the persons of elderly dowagers who were seen once a week at St. Peter's Church and then seen no more until the week again had passed.

Manor Road itself, and others like it, was surfaced with gravel and had no defined pavement edges, except that the pine trees did not grow in the central carriage way. They grew haphazard everywhere else, including the middle of the pavements. At the junctions with other roads were roundabouts, thickly overgrown with shrubs and trees and surrounded with iron railings. To get inside one of these islands was an adventure almost insupportably thrilling, especially as most pipe tobacco those days was sold in tins, and for some reason many such tins were thrown into the bushes. I was a great tobacco tin collector.

Along these tree-filled roads drove horse-carriages containing ladies dressed in black with great quantities of netting about their persons and wrinkles of skin hanging off their necks. Other ladies were dragged slowly along under the trees in wicker-work bath-chairs by bowed elderly gentlemen, *who could be hired at several street corners.* Think of that! And I am alive to remember it. There was even a bath-chair all shiny black, with a sort of flap over the occupant's knees, and drawn by a small horse!

All gone—old ladies, old gentlemen, bath-chairs, tree-filled islands, great houses, even the tobacco tins. One horse-cab lingered on for years, but I suppose so many ancient ladies died of sheer old age in it that the thing wouldn't do any more. Or perhaps it was the horse that died. And never in the whole of my life have I ridden in one of those wonders.

And the pier approach, with the old *Pier and Belle View Hotel,* and Sydenham's old-fashioned stationery shop, and the horse-trough and the almost rural quiet of Exeter Road and Westover Road! It was like walking in an old print. The Westover Cinema, a low white building, stood in its own garden with a front gate and shrubs, and a small notice board apologetically announcing that Rudolph Valentino was to be seen within. The rest of Westover Road consisted of villas in the Italian style, and banked up behind them were the tree-lined slopes of Upper Hinton Road, crowned with more villas,

including the residence of Sir Henry Taylor—dead, alas, long
before my time, and with him the greatest beard of the nine-
teenth century.

The town of Bournemouth has never cared for its literary
associations; this is not the place for an essay upon them, but a
small protest may be in order. Surely they merit a paragraph at
least in the lavish guide books which proclaim the excellence of
the town's bathing pools, cinemas, golf links and public
lavatories? In the churchyard of St. Peter's is buried the heart
of Percy Bysshe Shelley—is this not of general interest? It
might even be possible to charge twopence admission! The
house of Robert Louis Stevenson has been pulled down after
bombing, and a proposal to make a garden and some sort of
memorial fell through; so the curious visitor may inspect
instead a modern block of flats.

Sir Percy Shelley's house, Boscombe Manor, has fared better;
at least it is still there, and to its attractions have been added
a corrugated iron bicycle shed by the front door. The famous
private theatre, which some towns would unimaginitively have
used for theatricals, is being put to a sensible use at last. It is
full of lathes and other machinery where night-school scholars
can learn something of more use to them than poetry and such
nonsense. The folk who used to visit Stevenson—people like
Henry James—have left no mark on the streets of Westbourne
(sorry, avenues); and those who visited Sir Henry Taylor—
people like Tennyson—have left no mark where stand the
handsome blocks of luxury flats and the large expensive hotels
of the East Cliff. Sir Percy Shelley and his foolish amateur
theatricals are forgotten.

Now I had better get back to school. When brother Douglas
came to live with us (which, I suppose, was just after we moved
to 125) he and my sister went to St. Peter's School, and after a
term or two I followed. I was placed in Form II (Miss Plant).
For the next few years I was usually top of the form, except
sometimes when a little boy called Fred Lawrence was. Fred
Lawrence used to wear corduroy trousers which always had the

bottom button unfastened, and he lived in Christchurch Road. Another clever boy was Kenneth White, who is still clever, I believe, and a Librarian now somewhere in the Home Counties. His father managed (and perhaps owned, for I never knew) a grocery business near the Pembroke. That was the opposite way from where I lived and there was an odd sort of gulf between those pupils who lived west of the Square, and those who lived east. Not more than about half a dozen lived to the north; and of course just south of the schools was the sea. The only time I ever penetrated into the regions beyond the Square was on Saturday mornings sometimes when they had a thing called a "Kinemalogue", organised by the education authorities, at the Electric Theatre. I remember once the film shown was *Zeebrugge* and a man came on beforehand and sang a song called the Dover patrol, which to me seemed wholly irrelevant. He pronounced it "Dober".

That was about the time the mighty Wurlitzer Organs were coming in; it got in the end so that you couldn't go to see a picture in peace because these things kept on popping up out of the floor and imitating various other musical instruments. If anyone had installed an organ that sounded like an organ and nothing else, he would have made a fortune. Of course, going to the pictures these days is ten times worse, with several stops for meals in each performance, and about twenty minutes screen time to tell you not to miss next week.

We had a very poor football team at St. Peter's and I played for it once, the time St. Walburga's beat us nine-nothing. Cricket was not played at all. In that game against St. Walburga's the only time I had a chance to kick the ball our team captain Stanley Brushett kicked it first. So I kicked Stanley Brushett.

First Love

One day I found scribbled on the lavatory wall at school, "Eggy Hopkins loves Joan ————". On the whole, this intelligence pleased me. Most of my friends had sweethearts, and I had occasionally wondered if love had passed me by.

Before I explain why I was at that time called "Eggy"—for the person intended was undoubtedly me—I must define the steps by which I identified my charmer.

The "————" part of the legend I have not suppressed out of any feelings of delicacy, but because in the original that part had been obliterated by some work by another hand. My only clue, therefore, was the name Joan, and the school then contained at least three Joans, not counting one of the mistresses, whom I ruled out at once: she must have been at least twenty-six, and was said to be gone on Wiggy Bennett, the master.

An experienced lover would have inspected the three available Joans, and probably a Mary or two for good measure, before reaching a decision. But I was never really professional in my affairs, and I merely chose the one who happened to walk my way home from school.

I walked home with her perhaps twice, and we didn't get on very well together. However, being in love I found gave me some sort of status.

The extraordinary thing about one's schooldays, looking back at them through the mists of thirty years or so, is their unreality. Did I really regularly get two out of ten for spelling? Miss Plant once said there were some twenty-five thousand words in the vocabulary of Shakespeare, and that Hector Hopkins, so far as her class was concerned, probably came next with about three thousand. But as a matter of fact, I knew a number of others which I never used in her hearing—acute as it was.

My memories of school include a great many concerned with going home afterwards; I used to walk with a variety of little girls and boys, whose names and faces I cannot easily recall. One was called Elizabeth, and she lived in Waverley Road; another lived just round the corner in St. Swithun's Road, but I think here I can hardly have been in love, for I'm not at all sure that the St. Swithun's Road one wasn't a boy. Nobody in our road went to St. Peter's except my sister, my brother, and me. We seldom walked together, except sometimes on wet days, when we always met a gloomy woman who nodded hurriedly and said "Mucky day!" She rather reminded me of Cluey.

Now Cluey—not that I loved her—came long before Joan ————. I met Cluey when I was two. "What's your name, little boy?" she would ask: so they tell me, for I have forgotten. "My name's Louie," she would confide. "Cluey!" I would cry triumphantly.

She lived with Miss Pace, who gave me one violin lesson. "Every Good Boy Deserves Favour," my Mother used to say, "E.G.B.D.F., Eat Good Beef Dear Father." These phrases in some mysterious way were intended to fix certain musical rules in my mind; they failed. But their own absurd message is ingrained for life. Oddly enough, I have not the slightest idea what catch phrase was used for A, C, and the rest of the scale— if there is any more of it.

I cannot recall why I had only one violin lesson. I hope it was nothing to do with another strange thing that happened at this time, when I made my first attendance at Sunday School. Half way through the lesson the teacher looked at me with great meaning and asked if I didn't want to leave the room. I said, no, I didn't, and she said, I think you had better.

Now this happened at least thirty-five years ago, but I have never had an opportunity of discussing the thing until now. I want to make it quite clear that *I did not want to leave the room*. I think it was a little boy next to me,

Anyhow, I went, and soon afterwards I changed my religion.

Another thing I didn't like about that church was the way they ran their competitions. I went in for a drawing competition to draw a battleship, and I never even got an honourable mention. The prize went to a boy who had drawn a passenger liner, which shows what happens when women judge things. One of the women said my drawing was very pretty. Pretty! Those fifteen-inch guns were spouting death at the enemy, that great steel fabric was plunging in mountainous seas on a lee shore and none of the aeroplanes in sight had the least chance of ever reaching dry land again.

If Ada Allright ever reads this I want her to know that although we never spoke I used to watch her while we were sticking our gummed texts into albums and think how she was throwing herself away on the boy called Victor.

That was the East Cliff Congregational Church, and outside it in my day there was a cabmans' shelter and at least two horse-drawn cabs. The shelter has been cleared away now. It was an enchanting timbered little house lifted off the road at each corner on four bricks (perhaps only three on the offside) and underneath, I think, it had four iron wheels. I suppose if ever all the cabs were absent, at a pinch and in a real emergency the old man inside who used to fry bacon would have trundled off to pick up a fare with it. Even in those days I didn't somehow feel that a Congregational Church was the real thing, and soon after beginning to attend St. Peter's School I began going to the church. This, I thought, was the true religion and on one of the choir stalls there was a brass plate to say Mr. Gladstone had sat there, no doubt when resting from posting letters.

"Well, Heaven be thanked my first love fail'd," remarks Coventry Patmore, and if I echo him I hope Joan ——— as was (she is probably Joan * * * by now) will not be offended. She didn't want to do no better for herself than a boy in a black mackintosh.

And the coast was then clear for me to fall in love with Cecily Dawkins. I loved her passionately, but from afar. I fancy the only time we ever spoke was when I found a rose or a daisy in the gutter and as she passed she said, pointedly, "Pick up flowers, pick up sickness!" So I thought I had better not offer it to her.

Paul French loved her too, if I remember rightly. He used to cycle round in very small circles in the road outside her house. In those days I had no bicycle, and considered that he took a mean advantage. But then Paul made a practice of being in love with the same girls as the rest of us, and he made full use of his bike in the pursuit.

If writing poems means anything, the first girl I was ever in love with was Clarice. But in those Cecily Dawkins days I didn't even know of Clarice's existence.

And now for why I was called Eggy.

One day a girl at school whom I had never seen before, and indeed whom I cannot recollect ever seeing again, came up to me in the playground and began calling me Eggy-face. I think she had mistaken me for someone else, for the name could have had no physical basis; in those days I never ate eggs, nor for years after, as anyone will tell you: ask Paul, or Shindy.

No. I think the girl realized her mistake and went off to look for her friend somewhere else; but the damage was done and the name Eggy stuck to me until one day about twelve years later as we came up Cleveland Road towards Springbourne Library I told Paul I would be called Ken in future; and so the thing gradually passed over.

One of the odd things about children is their lack of curiosity about things an adult would investigate with interest. I used to walk to school quite often with a boy named Leonard Blake. We used to meet just about by East Cliff Church, our steps leading us more or less simultaneously to that point by about a quarter to two. Off we would go, usually along Littledown Road, kicking a ball or just talking. I never knew, and I shall now I suppose never know, where he came from before meeting me at East Cliff.

Another boy, whose very name I never knew, used to go to

St. Walburga's and if I went to school "down the town", that is by way of Old Christchurch Road, I would frequently see him going to his school by the same route, but whereas I would walk on the south side of the road, he would walk on the north. Every hundred yards or so one of us would shout a remark to the other across the road—commonplace remarks like "Holidays won't be long now" or "Roll on Saturday." This tenuous sort of relationship united us for years but after a while our paths ceased to cross and I have never seen him since. If we met now, what would we say to one another? "Up, St. Walburga's!" I suppose, or perhaps, "Roll on Saturday."

And another odd thing: this St. Walburga's—where was it? You went up a slope, I think, but in all the twenty-three years I lived permanently at Bournemouth, and in the seventeen since, I have never known exactly where it was; and I suppose it is gone now. For what ever survives that long in Bournemouth?

I Commence Author

I wrote my first poem at seven or eight and won the applause of Auntie Sally. Only the last two lines have survived (at least, I hope they are the last two, for anything more would have been an anti-climax):

> And there in the beer-cellar, where he had died,
> Lay the Butler, his throat slit, with fixed, horrid leer.

Auntie Sally, who had been in service all her life, thought very highly of this and said she had once known a Butler in similar circumstances. The poem displayed some powers of imagination, and a certain inherent appreciation of the laws of English prosody. I had never then—nor, I think, since—ever actually seen a butler alive or dead.

This poem, and several others written about that time, remained unprinted, although copied into a number of penny exercise books under the general title of *Poems, by Hector, Lord Hopkins*. I went so far as to explain to my mother once as we walked along Knole Road that I would one day be a famous man. For this day she is still waiting, and I confess so am I.

I must have been nearly ten before my first poem was published, and then I discovered that the Editor had been monkeying with my text. The poem was about a choir outing to Cheddar and in the course of it I remarked that we were so full of buns by lunch time that although the roast beef, etc., was very good we all refused a second helping. This circumstance I rendered into English verse very suitably, I thought, thus:

> But when offered some more, we mostly said no.

Now this happens to be an eleven-syllable line, and blank

verse requires but ten. So the editor quietly removed the word
"more" which made nonsense of the sentiment and did not
vitally improve the versification. And anyway Shakespeare
sometimes had eleven syllables, so why should not I?

I have gone into this at some length because many of these
Editors of Parish Magazines are little dictators, and after all it
isn't as if they were paying anything for the stuff. Another
thing was that I sent in a complete poem—a couple of hundred
lines, I dare say—and all that appeared was about twenty. I
bet he wouldn't have dared to do that to John Keble.

That was in 1924, I suppose. The parish magazine usually
appeared in church on a Sunday and that particular Sunday as
we came out after Matins I expected to see little knots of people
eagerly discussing the verses, and perhaps pointing out the
author to one another. Nothing of the kind. Nobody mentioned
them, although I hung about from one group to the next. All
that did happen—apart from me buying six copies—was that
weeks afterwards someone made a jesting reference to my
"effort"! Effort!—it cost me the minimum of labour, as a
matter of fact; for in those days I was a born poet and I used to
get perfection first time.

I appeared half a dozen times in the Parish Magazine in the
next ten years but made, I think, no further progress in my
calling until I put forth my *Twelve Poems* in 1936.

That choir outing comes, I suppose, under the heading
"treats" which would include Sunday School treats, choir
outings, and occasional educational trips from school (I say
"occasional" because there were about two in ten years, unless
you count that walk we once took with the Misses Alexander).
One of the school trips was to Southampton to view the docks,
ocean liners, etc., and only a couple of things about it seem
worth recording: (1) that in the bonded warehouses we saw leaf
tobacco stacked from floor to ceiling waiting its turn to be made
into cigarettes, which I thought highly remarkable, though I
forget why; and (2) that Bobby Rutter cut his ear. Now how
could a small boy cut his ear while inspecting the docks, ocean

liners, etc., in company with forty or fifty others and a number
of vigilant teachers?

Sunday School treats were nearly always held on wet days in
July. In the New Forest we used to pick foxgloves (I hope they
flower in July) and eat sweets from bags. The organised races
never seemed to come to much although I suppose the
prizes were given just the same. Egg and spoon was a favourite,
and sack races, and three-legged races. Looking back I am
bound to say I consider all these highly dangerous, and
certainly the teachers were careful never to take part. One
year when it rained particularly persistently we were all herded
into a large army hut behind the Balmer Lawn Hotel at
Brockenhurst and given an unlimited supply of buns and weak
tea. Another time we sat on Sway station for what seemed like
interminable hours waiting for a train which for some reason
never came. That was in the days of the old London and South
Western. I expect today it wouldn't come and you wouldn't be
allowed to sit and wait for it either, not all day. Another time
the Sunday School Treat was only to Poole, a mere tram ride.
We sat on the mud-beach somewhere by Parkstone Pier and
tormented small crabs. That time they had a tent in a field,
and also I believe a flag on a pole. I wonder if Sunday School
treats still go on, or if they were a Victorian survival?

The Sunday School went about in trains, but the choir
employed charabancs, another vehicle which had died as
completely as the horse cab; for the land-cruiser of today (as
they seem to call them) is not more completely different from the
old open chara than the radio-taxi is from the cab. I speak from
considerable experience, for my parents were great motor coach
trippers and we used to go off most Sundays in the summer, to
Cheddar, or Lulworth Cove, or the Forest, or Weymouth, or
Stonehenge. The charas were bright blue and yellow and
green and violet and orange and every shade of red, and there
were seemingly dozens of local companies doing a thriving
business. There was a row of doors along the side so that each
set of seats had its own entrance, and the passengers sat five or

six abreast. These sets were tiered one behind the other so that an uninterrupted view of the countryside was had by all; and the back seat was thus about twenty feet off the ground and you could sit in it and look into people's bedroom windows, or right over the roofs of cottages, haystacks and the like. Beside the driver sat a man with a sort of speaking trumpet pointing out marvels. And what marvels they were!—castles, battle-sites, bits of garbled local history, anecdotes, facetious remarks about people in rival charabancs, etc. One chap with whom we regularly travelled always pointed out a magnificent house in the Avenue, Branksome, as having been the home of Robert Louis Stevenson, where he wrote *Treasure Island, Ivanhoe*, and other famous works. This guiltless house was about half a mile from "Skerryvore", but the latter was difficult to see from the road, and stood on a nasty bend. So I suppose the chap thought he was acting for the best in enabling thousands of visitors to see a house they would otherwise have missed. Another favourite sight as we whizzed by was the house where Alfred burnt the cakes, and another was Woolbridge Manor House where Angel Clare spent "her" wedding night. By these means I became pretty knowledgable about local history; I know what Sir George Manners said when the gamekeeper told him his wife was in "The Baker's Arms", and I could take you now to at least three several cottages where (according to rival charabanc companies) William Rufus hid while escaping from Sir Walter Tyrrell—or vice versa.

One of the best excitements of these trips was putting the hood up. First we would dash along the Dorset lanes at breakneck speed in the hope of outpacing the storm, and finally we would have to stop because one or two ladies were pointedly pouring the water out of their laps. Then a couple of gentlemen in each row of seats (if any such there were) would stand up and pass the hood forward on its trellis supports until the driver could reach to tie it to the windscreen with a bootlace. Then out would come the sun and the yellow canvas hood would begin to steam and underneath it a curiously dungy smell would begin to circulate. While we stopped for tea at Corfe Castle ("twenty minutes here, ladies and gentlemen, and you can get a very nice cup of tea at the Olde Copper Kettle") the crew would safely restore the hood to its place hanging off the back, and the radiator would go off the boil.

Simple pleasures they seem now, but no doubt complex enough compared with those of my mother's youth. There is still in existence an old snap of her being trundled along in a bath-chair towed by a young man, in loud check knickerbockers and a boater, on a bicycle; and another in which my mother was not personally involved (but perhaps she held the camera), a bicycle made for three—or was it five—and ridden (propelled, I think is a better word) by three (or five) young men all so far as I remember exactly like the one with the bath-chair trailer. In those far-off days of the 'nineties they went about in horse-drawn brakes and places like Wallisdown (27 trolley-bus) were in the heart of the country. The world is continually getting smaller without, so far as I can see, getting correspondingly better. At Hurn, in the Rhododendron Forest, there is now a huge airport and it would be absurd for me to say I prefer rhododendrons. It was on the road near there, long before the days of the airport, that I once sat at three in the morning eating cucumber. I had long since learned that at three in the morning you sit where you can and eat what you can get, and if the occasion is graced with a flask of rum and coffee so strong that the spoon will stand upright in it, no harm will befall.

Another simple pleasure was going in the paddle steamer to Swanage. We used to exhibit a poster outside the shop and so we went for nothing now and again. Let me see, we had two paddle-steamer bills, and two cinema bills. The pass for the Westover was a neat little folding card, very discreet and chaste, which you showed at the door and so far as I remember (but surely I must be wrong?) they trusted you not to use more than once a week. The other was for a little picture house in Bos-combe, and on this one they used to make a cross in indelible pencil every time it was used. There were other advantages of having a shop; I remember my mother once acquired six nickel plated Apostle spoons by purchasing a hundred thousand meat cubes (probably a hundred thousand: I know they took several years to sell.)

For by this time my father's shoe repairing affairs had been shifted into the back room at 133 and in the front shop we had opened a grocery business. This was a pretty shrewd move, because there was no grocer between the top of the road, by East Cliff Church, and the Boscombe end which was ten minutes' walk away. Our part of Southcote road contained bigger houses than the station end, and none of those commercial yards backing on to the railway behind the houses. In fact we backed on to the tram depot, and the railway lay beyond that. So we felt (anyway, I did) that ours was a very select area.

Our house, 125, was one of a terrace of four, and joined on at the eastern end were two lock-up shops, the Post Office being the first and 133 the second. The Post Office sold newspapers, pens and pencils, sweets and tobacco—and of course stamps. It was kept by Mrs. Dawe whom for twenty years or so we called Mrs. Dawz without any protest from her. Excellent woman! She filled a large place in my infant life and doubtless my loud screams and other activities made some impact on hers. She lived at 129 and Miss Towser had her downstairs front room.

Now when our four houses were built about 1895 they were four shops; 127 was an off-licence, they do say; and the others were one thing and another. Then at some unspecified date the shop fronts were removed and front parlours put in. But of course the deeds allowed that formerly here had been shops, and my parents had no difficulty in getting 125 re-converted. So at last we finally gave up 133 (in which I ever retained a sort of proprietorial interest) and transferred everything to 125. And if anybody in those parts wants a packet of soap flakes or a pound of sugar they can be accommodated to this day, though their chances of meeting me hastily delivering the weekly orders in my soap-box-on-wheels have dwindled to vanishing point.

4

"Isn't he a lovely boy!" one lady used to say, but with less and less conviction as the years passed. In the end even I grew too big for a soap box and we got a delivery-cycle with a basket on the front and "E. Hopkins, Grocer" on the side. This cycle had a back-pedalling brake and I got extremely skilful at applying this in such a manner on the wet wood-block surface of Old Christchurch Road that I could go most of the way from the Lansdowne to the Square sideways, crab-like, without falling off. Believe me, this was a miracle.

One obvious result of our opening a shop was that we ceased to buy our groceries from T. Curtis or from Lickfold's.

T. Curtis had almost the smallest shop I ever saw, and he was himself one of the largest men in my experience (but I was then pretty small and perhaps he wasn't really so very large.) Anyhow he and one customer more than filled the shop. He used to sell a confection called Ogo-Pogo Eyes, which was a sort of gob-stopper. "Ogie-Pogies" he used to call them, which annoyed me. I was inclined to be precise in such things. In the end I began to buy my Ogo-Pogo Eyes elsewhere where they were called by their proper name.

Final Reminiscences before attaining the Age of Fourteen

In those days you left school at fourteen and went out to work; but before taking this step and describing my impact upon the labour market I must dispose of a few clergymen and others.

As a choir boy I had excellent opportunities for observing clergymen, and I must say at once that this section of the community has always fascinated me. I must have known scores of them, mostly pale young curates at first, but towards the end quite a few Canons, and at least one Dean (if you count him getting made Dean after I ceased to know him).

I drifted into being a choir boy. One day Miss Plant said we had to go to the church and be interviewed by the choirmaster; so off we went and the next thing I knew I was a choir boy. I was bottom boy on the Cantoris side with an uninterrupted view right down the church to the font and the Rev. C. R. Rockett sitting behind me. Directly opposite sat the Rev. Lumley Green Wilkinson, a much less formidable figure who never fiercely snapped his fingers at us. Mr. Rockett did, and produced a noise like a pistol shot which used to terrify the Decani over the way. There was also a choir-man, Arthur Davis, who used to look fierce sometimes, and as he got older grew to look fierce all the time, at the Decani. Luckily they had no champion on their side to glower at us, but once to the dismay of every single boy, and of not a few men, Mr. Trench said out loud in the middle of the service, "Edgar Wilson, go to the Vestry!" How extremely small a choir-boy can look if he walks out by himself, and goodness how red in the face! How the singing redoubled when the time to sing came again!

This Mr. Trench shared with me the nickname "Eggy"; but as he was thoroughly bald, he had a better title to it. He was a humane man, I think. At all events, I once saw a look of despair cross his face when he trod on a caterpillar in the chancel on his way to preach.

These caterpillars we used to employ in races from one side to the other; we also used to race a kind of bee which had its hive in the grassy banks of the churchyard.

In my day it was some choir. Eighteen boys, we had, and about fourteen men (stalls for twelve and any extras on chairs). But on great days when certain ancients appeared I have seen the men extend almost into the sanctuary and Mr. Chandler has pedalled away at the organ like one possessed and the whole church has shaken with the singing. My years as a choir-boy gave me the thorough grounding in the Psalms which I retain to this day, as the company in various Fleet Street taverns can testify. "God is gone up with a merry noise," we used to sing, "and the Lord with the sound of the tru-hump!"

It was now that Miss Critchley (who really went to St. Swithun's) made a pilgrimage to St. Peter's in order to report that I looked like a little angel. I probably did. We wore light blue cassocks and nice white surplices; the men wore black cassocks and white surplices, and the servers on special occasions wore red cassocks and surplices trimmed with lace. *On Sundays we wore Eton suits and mortar boards.* None of that sort of thing now, alas. The first Eton suit I had came from Hope Brothers and I went along to buy it alone. Apparently you had to try them on, a necessity new to me. The man shut me in a little room with the suit and left me to undress! but he kept on popping in. I was very shy, and this perhaps explains why my first Eton suit was not a perfect fit. I said it would do nicely when I had only tried on the jacket.

Curates were much less permanent than choir-boys; I saw a succession of them come and go; even "Squibby" Rockett departed in the end, snapping his fingers to the last. Time was when St. Peter's sustained nine curates and a Vicar, and they all lived in St. Peter's Vicarage overlooking the sea—so it is said. But that's a hundred years ago. In my day two seemed to be the ration, and one of these seldom appeared because he was charged with administering the branch establishment at St. Swithun's. Most of the Bournemouth churches stemmed originally from St. Peter's, which was the first church in those parts; and accordingly I used rather to look down upon the people who elected to worship at St. Michael's, or St. Ambrose. Poor relations of a sort, they seemed to me. As for St. Swithun's that still "belonged" to us and the choir-boys there could really do little except when we went along two or three times a year and lent a hand. St. Swithun's had no tower, either.

There is a Christmas card which crops up most years in one form or another depicting a group of little angels in cassocks and surplices singing lustily under a bit of holly, or perhaps a pair of bells. One of them has his mouth particularly wide open, and this is me. I used to be in a strong position to open my mouth wider than the others, because I wasn't singing. The only time I could be relied upon to produce a piercing note was in that pregnant bit of the Hallelujah chorus right at the end when everyone else stopped. "Eeek!" I used to go.

We should have been good: we had ten services a week and four practices. We were paid three-ha'pence a time for each attendance, and two shillings or half-a-crown for weddings and funerals. As most of my readers probably don't go to church as often as that I had better explain how this great total was arrived at. The practices were on Monday, Tuesday and Thursday for us boys, and for the men as well, on Friday. Then on Monday, Tuesday, Thursday, Friday and Saturday we had evensong at five-thirty. On Friday at five-past-twelve we sang the litany. On Sunday we sang eucharist at ten, matins at eleven-fifteen, "first" evensong at three and choral evensong (i.e., men too) at six-thirty. In addition, on saint's days we sang eucharist at eleven, and of course all sorts of extra activities at Easter, Christmas, and so on.

In my first years as a choir-boy there was a "choir-boys home" at which a number of boys from other towns who desired the unspeakable privilege of singing with me and the other local

chaps were accommodated under the benevolent despotism of
Mr. and Mrs. Dear. One of these boys (it usually seemed to be
Billie Sinton) was charged with the duty of taking a hot dinner
on a plate and under a piece of cloth from the home, in Old
Christchurch Road by Dalkeith Steps, to Mr. Webber's house
in Southcote Road. He used to get a penny for the tram each
way, and thus a certain tram daily (or perhaps only a couple of
times a week) used to be filled unaccountably with the aroma of
roast beef or a grilled chop. But what I never fathomed was,
what happened to the dirty plates? Billy Sinton never took them
back, he used merely to deliver them full and hot, or cold if he
happened to have walked and spent the penny. I suppose there
is some quite simple explanation to all this, but I shall never
know it.

Mr. Webber's father, Alderman Webber, figured in an
incident which my brother Douglas was heard to recount to
Dr. Scorer. About 1923 there was some sort of small-pox scare
and everyone had to be vaccinated and wear a thick bandage on
the arm surmounted with a bit of red ribbon to warn the
others not to jog into him.

So we were taken round to Dr. Scorer, my sister, my brother,
and me, to be done, and Douglas, who was about thirteen and
able to talk casually as man to man with people, an accomplish-
ment I had not yet thoroughly acquired, asked the Doctor if he
knew what Alderman Webber had done once when a crisis
arose in the Council?—he had threatened to vaccinate his seat!
After we got home there was another crisis because my mother
didn't think Douglas ought to have said such a thing, even if it
was true.

Looking back I see a long procession of clergymen attached
to the rear end of the choir as it makes its way from the vestry,
through the north transept and into the chancel, old Harry
Crumpler going in front with the Cross. Of course these
clergymen were not all there at the same time, but it seems so
now. Mr. Feast, young Mr. Banks, Mr. Lewin, Mr. Blake,
Mr. Scarlen, the Revs. Rockett and Trench aforementioned,

and of course the several vicars of my time—Mr. Green Wilkinson, Canon Burrows, Canon Marsh, and Canon Williams.

Mr. Scarlen appears and disappears, leaving behind in my memory only his odd way of repeating prayers: "Nour Father," he used to begin. He took a photograph of me which confirms Miss Critchley's estimate of my personal appearance at the age of ten.

Mr. Green Wilkinson I once somewhat disconcerted by the Lytch Gate by asking him if he liked me. I daresay he had never even noticed me before. Anyway, after not too long a pause he said yes.

Silvery-haired Mr. Lewin we all liked; he lived in a cottage at the top of the Churchyard, the lodge, I suppose, to Sir Henry Taylor's old house—or the house next door. He became Vicar of Burton, the village on the edge of the forest, beyond Christchurch, where Robert Southey once lived (and I didn't get that from a charabanc guide).

But my best friend among them all was Canon Marsh—because he became vicar when we were growing up and were able to appreciate his unique qualities.

By this time I had long since graduated from Miss Plant's Form II and after varying spells in III, IV and another short-lived form called "Remove", had passed finally through V into VIb, which came more or less directly under the headmaster's eye. VIa, the grandest of all, I never reached because I got to the age of fourteen first. Anyway, all they did in VIa was sit at different desks once a week to learn "French", and I don't suppose they could have sustained much of a conversation with André Maurois at the end of it all. I still knew the most English words in the school!

The days when Wiggy Bennett could ask my sister if she happened to know if I had washed my ears that morning had long passed. I was now a sub-prefect, with no powers beyond the wearing of a small badge, and quite an important citizen in other ways. I had risen from bottom place in the choir to third or fourth from the top, and was something of a favourite with the assistant-organist, Miss Cutler—with whom I was a little in love, I thought. I was also now a Boy Scout; only a Tenderfoot its true (and I was never anything else) but at least I was now empowered to wear a number of items of official dress: my Eton suit for Sundays, my Scout dress for Wednesday evenings, and my sub-prefect's badge all the rest of the week. I was also about to become a member of St. Peter's Players but unfortunately there wasn't any badge for that.

Formation of Character, Learning to ride a Bicycle, etc.

I do not recommend myself as a model for other children. Almost as soon as I could talk I said to my sister that the way to get what one wanted was to "keep on, like I do!" And my mother says my keeping-on was interminable. However, it took me about seven years to get a bicycle, and then I had to buy it myself for 3s. Previous to this I had to be content with shuffling along in the gutter with Porky's, which was too large for me to ride. Every Sunday after Matins a crowd of us would walk home together, the others in conversation and me a hundred yards or so ahead shuffling with the bike. Porky's other excellence lay in the provision of paper for me to draw on.

This was foolscap typewriting paper which Porky used to give me in quite large handfuls from the office where he worked. I never could fully understand that office. It was the local branch of a famous furniture stores, and it had no furniture for sale, no proper shop even, simply a sort of shed by the railway in which was Porky giving out the firm's stationery. I suppose there was postal business, or something; but I for one wasn't surprised when the branch closed down and Porky went elsewhere to work.

The first book I ever chose for myself, apart from that school prize which was the best of a bad job, anyway, was Creasy's *Fifteen Decisive Battles* aforementioned. I cannot exactly date this occasion but I was already old enough to know that threepence is a fair price for most secondhand books. I chose Creasy from a tray outside a junk shop in Boscombe—now vanished—and my mother paid the threepence. This purchase I never regretted.

This was probably before I made a bookcase at "Woodwork".

Woodwork was not one of my favourite studies; in fact I distinctly disliked it, and I was afraid of the master, who used to throw pieces of wood and even hammers. He had an assistant-master who usually stood prudently behind him wearing a half-smile. I suppose if any boy were stunned he was able to broaden it in no time.

I made three things at woodwork during the six or eight terms I attended the class (it was held at Bournemouth School, a posh affair which you paid to go to.)

The first thing I made was a knife box, with two long divisions (forks and knives) and one short, going crossways (spoons). Owing to a misunderstanding this last division would accommodate no spoon more than three inches long, and in the end I believe my mother used it for small nails and drawing pins. I had used for this contraption timber about an inch thick, and it was provided with a large iron handle for lifting. Stained a vivid green, it was worth at term-end every one of the three out of ten marks it obtained.

Then I made my masterpiece, a destroyer, with two funnels, two masts (one higher than the other), guns, searchlights and all. The teachers prudently left me to get on with this piece of naval architecture, and by the time all was done and I had painted it battleship grey it was a pretty handsome affair. It never floated, but I had it for years on the mantelpiece in my bedroom.

The bookcase was much simpler in conception: in fact, it consisted of three long pieces of wood dovetailed into two short pieces, the whole painted white. It held seventy books.

We had very few books at home until I began to buy them. There was a thick cookery book, a copy of *In Memoriam* in limp leather, *Mrs. Halliburton's Troubles*, a handsome Bible also in limp leather, and a few books my brother had brought from Rochester. To these may be added the books given to my sister or me at odd times, but nothing I particularly remember.

However, the book-buying habit was strong in me from the first and I soon added to Creasy. I bought a three-volume

Bible in quarto for threepence and carried it triumphantly but breathlessly to church where it created a sensation in the vestry. I think the Curate thought I meant to read it during the sermon. But it was only on its way home, and once there I think was never looked at again. This came from Commins, an establishment of which I have since been a satisfied customer for thirty years. From Draytons, the other principal local bookshop, I acquired my first copy of *Mr. Midshipman Easy*, all by myself, and I like to think that I recognised it for a classic even then. I know it was a wholly vile edition, printed badly on poor paper and it cost me 7*d*. From the Boscombe bookshop, Wright's, I bought the *Collected Poems* of A. C. Benson (3*s*.) and here and there about the town almost a dozen other titles by this author. I thought he must be "literature" because he used to say "sate" for "sat", and had a number of similar refinements of style not hit upon by his fellows. I only failed to buy a first edition of Dante because Paul and I rushed to the library after seeing it for sixpence to make sure it was the Dante we had heard of; it was, but we learned incidently at the same time that the first edition proper is in Italian and appeared some five hundred years before the copy we had examined. So much for Dante! But that's the way to learn.

I used to buy books I'd heard of, or books by authors I'd heard of, and take them home and sample them. In this way I read a mass of miscellaneous stuff and by the age of sixteen I had acquired what Lord Cockburn calls "a respectable chaos of accidental knowledge". Let me see: A. C. Benson, Rabelais, *Gallions Reach*, Flecker, the novels of Ford Maddox Hueffer, M. R. James's Ghost Stories, a whole lot of Chesterton, Baring and Belloc, and James Stephens's *Deirdre*, my first edition of which was worth (someone told me) ten pounds. This was not so, but never mind. The battle scenes alone are worth ten pounds to keep it on the shelf, and there my copy still is.

Useful advice was forthcoming at this time from John Dent, whose advantage of some five or six years, and his commanding position on the public library staff, plus the authority that always accompanies the smoking of a pipe, all served to establish him as an expert. It was he who told me Alice Meynell ought not to be missed, and who first drew Flecker to my attention.

I became a good customer at the library, although one of the lady assistants once annoyed me by enforcing the rule that you can't borrow a book and return it on the same day. I read in the course of a year or so every book they possessed on Arctic exploration; a vast quantity of stuff about the naval war, 1914–1918; all the books on Egyptian antiquities; and a lot of literary criticism by George Saintsbury—who is certainly the best critic to put into the hands of a growing lad.

Another discovery I made at the age of ten or eleven was that you could go into the Reference Library and sit down and read *Punch* in bound volumes going back donkey's years. I used to ask importantly for *Punch*, 1871, and get it without any fuss in its thick blue cloth case (it usually comes in red, but there is a blue issue, too.)

All this literature made me feel mighty superior to people whose reading barely extended beyond *Bindle* or *If Winter Comes*. I went one day into Draytons at Westbourne and enquired if they had Sterne's *Sentimental Journey*. "Is that her latest?" asked the young lady, and on this little story I dined out for the rest of the winter. I got into the habit of asking for impossible books: "I wonder if you happen to have the 1707 edition of Prior?" They probably thought I was a little touched; and what would have happened if they had produced a copy and asked for thirty pounds I can't imagine.

However, the habit stood me in good stead on at least one occasion. During the war, when I was stationed at Witney, I thought I would take the opportunity of reading at the Bodleian, so off I went to apply for a ticket. How my size nine army boots rang on the ancient floors of Duke Humphrey's library! Bodley's librarian, or one of his chaps, received my form of application and proceeded to enquire what impediment prevented my using the public library. I was studying the minor poets of the seventeenth century, I affirmed. Ah, such as what? *I then by sheer luck named a book of which there is no copy in the Bodleian.* All after this was plain sailing; indeed they almost begged me to make use of what few poor volumes they had been able to gather and I verily believe I could have carried a couple of armsful away. So I got my ticket and about a week later I was posted to Northampton. I hope my non-reappearance didn't make them think I was angry with them.

In Brussels a year or so later I made occasional use of the Royal Library and esteemed myself thereby a scholar of international repute, familiar with the world's great collections, and on Christian name terms with the custodians of Folger, Rylands, Huntingdon and the rest.

I hope I was not so impertinent as to tell any of the officials that it was a pleasant little library. One lesson it took me long to learn was when to keep silent; I suppose I have yet to master it fully. Paul and I were once shown all the treasures and points of interest in Fordingbridge Church by a gentleman who was either the local magnate or the vicar's warden: perhaps both. He may indeed have been the patron of the living. Anyway, we offered him sixpence.

Life is singularly complicated. On another occasion, when some sort of offering would have been in order—after my marriage—I was going off without making it, and I had to be run after.

I Become a Builders' Merchant

I suppose there can be no harm in saying that I was apprenticed to Holts. They will doubtless long since have forgiven me.

H. J. Holt Ltd., Builders' Merchants, had their head offices and stores at Southampton, but they had various branch establishments, of which the imposing corner premises in Holdenhurst Road was one. To this firm on leaving school at fourteen I was bound apprentice for four years, beginning at five shillings a week. They for their part undertook to teach me the trade of builders' merchant, to which was added ironmongery, paints and wallpapers, garden tools and sundries, household goods, gas and electrical fittings, and a whole lot more. I undertook to be punctual, honest, hardworking, not to swear or seduce my master's daughter, etc. All this printed on a form with blanks for my name and theirs, and a sixpenny stamp. I have the document somewhere still.

I believe I was not wholly unsuccessful in this trade. I dusted and swept diligently, using wet sawdust for the later operation under the guidance of Mr. Holt himself. "Don't sprinkle it about," he told me, "but push it along in a line, driving the dust before it." This I always did on the days he was visiting us from Southampton. "Eyup!" my fellow apprentice John used to cry, "the Old Man!" And down would go a neat line of wet sawdust in skirmishing order.

John's real name was Kenneth, but they didn't hold with fancy names. Me they called William.

It was from John that I bought my first bicycle for 3s. and a nice little machine it was. I rode it for two or three years.

One of our jobs was to cycle round once a week and deliver invoices and statements to the customers; we each took half the town and off we would go with perhaps a couple of hundred envelopes to deliver. I got to know every street and alley for five miles round and now, twenty years and more afterwards, I could tell you the quickest way from Richmond Wood Road to Terrace Road. Not that I ever went the quickest way myself.

In those four years I learnt quite a lot about the honourable trade of ironmongery. I learned the difference between Berlin, Brunswick and Lamp Black, and how all these differed from Black Japan (though not why in this last case the order of words is reversed.) I learned the use of water-gas-tar, and not to leave the boiled-oil tap dripping. And what a lot of things there are to know the names of!—cleat hooks, S hooks, cantilever brackets, hooks and rides, brass butts, copper disc rivets, and lost-head screws. I learned to speak of cane-and-white sinks, pedestal pans, Siraphite, Portmadoc slates and wire-cut bricks, and quarries, and Sankey down-draught-preventers, and Knoxall track and small-hammered glass, and scrim and tow and plasterers' hair.

I could take a lawn-mower to pieces.

I also knew a secret way of working the lift without closing the doors, and it is a mercy I was never electrocuted.

John was much cleverer than me. He could put a lawn-mower together again. And he could cut keys and mend locks and repair vacuum-cleaners. So they gave me the unskilled labour, like weighing-up nails—or, worse, making bundles of wire wall-ties, an almost impossible task because they persist in all pointing different ways and they are devilish sharp.

After a year or so another apprentice came, and to him John and I transferred a load of wet sawdust and the fishing rights in the wire wall-ties bin. But the delivery of invoices we carefully guarded. It meant a full day out in the public streets every week and a pile of envelopes that looks tremendous can be delivered in about an hour if you cycle like a maniac, as we did. After that

John, I think, used to go swimming. My mecca was the book-shops or the public library.

The new apprentice I named Pliny; and sometimes we varied this by calling him Aristotle. His real name was Harold.

We had half a dozen assistants in the shop, and the store-men (whom we looked down on, rather: there was also a store-boy, whom we looked down on very markedly. Alfie; I suspect that as a Builders' Merchant he was worth the whole lot of us.) Then we had a delivery-boy and two lorries complete with drivers, one of whom was so short-sighted that he was con-stantly carrying away the sides of half-built houses and backing into lime-pits and so on.

What the assistants thought of me I don't know; only one—Fred—had any faith in my powers of poetry. I told him one day I had now written seventeen sonnets—one more than Keats. I think I must have calculated from an edition that was defec-tive. I admitted that a few of mine were probably not up to his standard, but he was twenty-seven and I was barely sixteen. Let him wait awhile!

I also counted as sonnets certain fourteen-line poems in rhyming couplets; several others in blank verse; and at least one which on a recount was found to have only thirteen lines. Poetry is an exacting mistress, especially when wooed in intervals of weighing up three-inch cuts.

It was about this time that I went out with one of the lorries to help the driver unload and at one stop I hung my jacket on the tailboard. It didn't survive the journey and I never saw it again. In the inside pocket were several of my latest and best sonnets. So if anyone picked up a grey tweed jacket somewhere in the West Cliff area of Bournemouth about midsummer, 1930, with several rather good sonnets in the inside pocket, it was mine. I should like to add those to the canon; but I had no copies. I will choose a specimen from the survivors and risk the verdict that in the past quarter of a century my work had got steadily worse.

SONNET

Now am I well content, the worst has passed;
As when through rare and tiny rifts I see
The sky show blue 'mid thunder cloud and rain,
And seeing, I rejoice; my soul set free
Wings fearless through the tempest toward the sun.
Or, as a man imprisoned underground
Beholds the door unlocked and standing wide,
Freeing the way to life and liberty,
So am I filled with hope and dawning joy
And set my stumbling footsteps toward the light.
Once I was dumb—but now my tongue speaks fire;
Once I was blind—I now behold the stars;
Though I was lonely, now I weep no more;
Though I was weary, now my spirit sings.

Paul and I thought highly of this and Paul said Joyce Honeywill had said in a hushed sort of voice, it is poetry.

"If a man believes he is worshipping God," says Ernest Thompson Seton, "he *is* worshipping God." Perhaps this is true of a lad of seventeen who believes he is writing poetry.

At the end of my four years' apprenticeship I left Holts and went to Middletons. Middletons was a smaller firm and there were five of us—Mac, Mr. Mead, Fred the driver, me, and a girl clerk who frightened me. Oh, and the manager, who was also the traveller if I remember rightly. The premises were extraordinary: we had a conventional shop-front behind which were a series of barn-like buildings of which we occupied an upper floor only: the downstairs being a garage. Most of our goods were paints, wallpapers, and such like; and glass. I soon learned to cut glass and became so proficient that I used to cut large fancy shapes for practice while waiting for customers. This can hardly have assisted the glass department to show a profit.

It was while I worked at Middletons that I first visited the shining city of London. The firm had been taken over by a big London concern and now and again Fred used to go there with the lorry to collect supplies. One day I begged leave to accompany him, and Mac found specially in favour because he

5

wanted me to see where he had worked in his grand days, that is at the old-established city house of Pryke and Palmer. I never subsequently passed along Upper Thames Street without thinking of Mac and his constant cry: "When I was with Pryke and Palmers . . ." Excellent McCabe, you were the nicest ironmonger I ever knew.

So Fred and I departed in the orange-painted van, through the Forest, through Winchester, and over Hartley Flats, where Paul said the Lagonda had once touched eighty—or perhaps ninety, I forget. Fred and I did about fifty-three and nearly shook ourselves to pieces. We came in along the embankment and I pointed out the sights to Fred—here the River Thames, and there the Houses of Parliament. He was surprised at the extent of my knowledge of the place, and so was I. But of course I had been looking at a picture of the Houses of Parliament for years on the sauce bottle at home; and if that wasn't the Thames, then the Fleet Ditch was in flood!

At last we reached Norton Folgate, the oddly-named street of our destination, and Fred magnanimously stated that from now on my time was my own till six o'clock. I found a policeman and asked to be directed to Charing Cross Road.

The next time I visited London was a year or so later with Paul and Phyllis in the M.G. That day Hartley Flats came into their own. Once we were in London I sent Paul and Phyllis off to amuse themselves and settled down to renewing acquaintance with the now tolerably familiar streets. Towards evening I took a snack in a milk bar in Panton Street and leaning confidentially over the counter said knowingly to the chap, "Many people in town?" but he didn't seem to know. Probably some provincial lured to the metropolis by visions of big money. I left him to it.

It was about this time that I was spoken to by a girl, to my infinite terror. I had heard of such things, and I expected to be robbed, beaten-up, and left for dead in a dark entry. "Love to, but no money!" I gasped, blushing brightly and appreciably quickening my pace. I got back into the whirl of Piccadilly

Circus as quickly as I could and left the fringes of Soho to the policemen patrolling in twos. When I carefully described this incident to Paul later he said with a great air of wisdom, "Glasshouse Street isn't any good!"

And I went to the pictures.

Meanwhile I was becoming a real expert in my line: I'd had five years of it now and I could discuss pantiles, and steel casements and water-waste-preventers with anybody.

I can't recall exactly why I got the sack from Holts, although I know my mother went round about it. In the same way, my leaving Middletons is shrouded in mystery after all these years. I left with the august names of Pryke and Palmer sounding in my ears and went to work for Hooper and Ashby. For those who like statistics of the kind, I think I may say that Hooper and Ashby had nine branches and probably thirty lorries. We also had back doors opening directly on to the railway sidings, and I used to go out and uncouple trucks and push them about as if I were a railwayman. Of course we never had an engine up our bit of line, but all the same the thing was a distinct advance on Middletons where we only had a trap door with a pulley.

But I had sunk to the status of yard-boy! I worked under a foreman, and the girls in the office hardly looked at me. The chaps called me Ken but the office clerks called me Hopkins, all except Ducky, who still I believe sometimes asks after me kindly although it is all of twenty years since I got the sack.

Another of the office chaps discovered that I wrote poetry and begged leave to look. I lent him a bulky exercise-book full—the same, I think, that I later sent to W. B. Yeats. Mr. Blench—that was his name—returned the book and made no comment beyond a civil thank you. I excused him to myself by concluding he found the work too advanced for him. As for W. B. Yeats, he didn't answer.

Utterpug The Terrible

I find listed at the end of *Utterpug the Terrible, a tragedy of elemental passions in two acts* nine other plays by the same hand. The hand was mine.

At least two of these plays were staged (if you count the vicarage lawn as a stage; otherwise, only one). Of most of the rest I remember nothing, except that *For the King*, a spy drama, could only be produced in a theatre able to mount, among other props, a Bentley "rocketing and streaming through the night" at ninety miles an hour (I suppose at a pinch eighty would have done). But the real impediment to production, Procky told me, was the fact that although the play was divided into three acts it would play for only twenty minutes. This seems to be a common defect in young dramatic authors. Someone—I am almost certain it was Tommy Earp—told me his first play met similar objections. But he was only eleven; I was nineteen and old enough to know better. So that was the last of *For the King*.

Before describing the triumphant production of *Utterpug the Terrible* I must say something about St. Peter's Players, that redoubtable dramatic club. We had a chap who played Robertson Hare parts just right, and another who was excellent in Ralph Lynn rôles. How lucky that yet a third talented member could impersonate Tom Walls!

None of these members was me. I played Baki in *Ask Beckles*, the lift boy in *Leave it to Psmith* and a dead body under the sofa in act one of a play I forget the name of; I didn't see much of it. And I was a pretty bloodcurdling scream once in *A Night at an Inn*. For the rest I showed people to their seats, fetched beer, etc.

It was about this time that I formed hopeless attachment

68

for a succession of girls who played various leading parts. José, Sylvia—dear me, there were several more and I can't even remember their names. They were mostly on rather friendly terms with one or two Players who had cars. A leading lady, I suppose, cannot be expected to go home on the back of the bike of the body in act one.

If I cannot recall those talented, lovely, and unattainable darlings, at least I will write down the names of a group of consummate drinkers—(let none of them object to the phrase: it is from a 15th-century poem—literature, therefore, and allowed to stand). These included George Cookman, K. K. Procter, Alan Powell, Jack Backhurst, Shindy and me. Yes, I could put it away with the best in those days; a laggard in love, perhaps, but one of the first there when the Cri. opened.

Oh, my companions, scattered, lost or dead! Certain other drinkers stand now in the pubs we knew! Lost to me for ever the bars of the Grand and the Cri., the soft musicks of the Norfolk, the discreet dim lights of the Highcliffe, the roaring Grill of the Pembroke, the sanded floor of the Pembroke Shades, the Pavilion where we called for pickled onions, and the Royal and the Lansdowne and the Fox. Just as well, for I couldn't afford it now. And—"what has been, has been, and I have had my hour!" ("Ay, several hogsheads, I'll warrant you!")

Well, of course, with people like Ian Hay, and Wodehouse, and Ben Travers at call, there was no real demand for my three-act plays. But at a Vicarage Garden Party, when everyone was in a tolerant mood, and so long as I didn't insist on too many of the stars taking part, there might be an opening for a local playwright.

Accordingly, on June 5, 1935, *Utterpug the Terrible* was first (and last) played, with the following attractive cast:

Otherwiggle the Craven	Alan Powell
Felicia the Winsome	Christina Stevens
Utterpug the Terrible	F. Frankland Rigby

Ferdinand the Bard	Patrick Dear
Roger Wrynek the Ridiculous	Cyril Jacobs
Turgid the Bold	Knighton Proctor
Old Moore	Victor Newton

the unexpected last minute non-arrival of Miss Stevens, detained on business in Nottingham, left the producer H. K. Hopkins no alternative but to play the heroine himself.

I won't summarise the plot because so far as I can see there isn't one, but I will give specimens of the dialogue which I confess (reading the play today for the first time for twenty years) I find at once surprising and eloquent.

(*Act One, in which battle has just been joined.*)

OTHERWIGGLE.

    I will take me to the conflict and there abide: it will be my glorious duty to hover in the rear of the battle, ready to fling myself to any danger spot I may see. I may then snatch a brief sleep, careless of danger, in some pig-sty or behind a hedge. Nor will I hesitate to run messages, so only they be to the rear of the battle. Ha! One cometh!

    (*Enter a soldier, running. He is sore wounded.*)

FELICIA.

    What news, thou man of war?

SOLDIER (*never pausing*).

    They have seized the City Mangle!

FELICIA (*swooning*). [I had to be very careful not to fall off the tower—a pair of steps.]

    Ah, merciful Jove protect us!

OTHERWIGGLE (*catching her*).

    Be strong my hand to save her!

    (*A second warrior staggers in and falls dead*)

I believe on the day the second warrior would only have been forthcoming by a drastic depleting of the audience; so we used the same one twice. Luckily he had just time to stagger off the first time and change his helmet.

I won't trace the fortunes of this drama minutely, but I ought to add that half-way through the battle scene the Vicarage dog appeared and bit Turgid the Bold.

Here are the dying speeches of the two principal heroes:

TURGID.

> If one of you will support me, I will make my dying
>   speech.
> A Turgid Ho! My dying throat
> Flings the dread challenge over the moat!
> A Turgid Ho! In accents weak
> My cry rings out across the creek!
> A Turgid Ho! The echoes fall
> Impotently against the wall!
> A Turgid Ho! A Turgid Ho!
> Let me repeat before I go,
> My battle cry: A Turgid Ho!
> Wherever warriors congregate
> My fame is known, my name is great,
> And dying, I shall leave behind
> A name remembered, and men shall find
> Mention of me wherever they go,
> And—may I repeat it?—A Turgid Ho!
> Turgid I lived and Turgid I died,
> And be it remembered, it was my pride,
> Whenever I chanced a-fighting to go,
> To bellow aloud: A Turgid Ho!
>   Put me down gently, lass. (*Expires.*)

ALL.

> Jolly good! Hooray!

UTTERPUG.

> Hold me up quickly, someone! I've got one!
>   (*They support him.*)

A thousand times I've conquered, and a thousand times
the foe
Beneath my sword Exbatterpate have been brought very
low;
Ay, men for miles around have cringed at mention of my
name
For UTTERPUG THE TERRIBLE is not unknown to fame!
I too am mentioned with respect as far away as Poole,
A most barbaric neighbourhood, avoided as a rule,
But even there, ay! even there, "An Utterpug!" they cry
When they behold my banners and my warriors pass by.
An Utterpug! An Utterpug! What name on earth more
feared,
By ladies more remembered or by schoolboys more
revered?
An Utterpug! Ah, noble name! An Utterpug! Hooray!—
But Utterpug the Terrible, he too must pass away;
My time is come; my end is near; let my grave eke be dug;
But ere I go, may I remark, Yo Ho! An Utterpug!
Cheerio, you lot. (*Expires.*)

OTHERWIGGLE.

So perish all such.

FELICIA.

What do you mean by that?

OTHERWIGGLE.

Nothing; but it sounds appropriate.
"So perish all such"—and that goes for my play.

I had, as a matter of fact, no great ambition to write plays. I
was content to be a poet—a master of the sonnet. This rather
choice phrase I borrowed from a lady who lived in Winton.

One day at the library I had come upon a book called
Lessons in Verse Craft by S. Gertrude Ford and I discovered
somehow that Miss Ford was a local author (I had thought I
was the only one, because with splendid arrogance I didn't
count Major P. C. Wren.) Frankly, I didn't expect Miss Ford

to be able to teach me anything, but I thought if I drew her attention to myself I might get a bit of praise. So I cycled over to Winton and tracked down her house and boldly rang the bell. Miss Ford was not at home, but I had some conversation with another lady who asked me all about myself. I said I was a poet and I wrote sonnets. "Miss Ford is an acknowledged mistress of the sonnet," observed the lady who answered Miss Ford's door. I never went there again, scenting a rival perhaps, or fearing to lose a couple of my best lines.

About the same time I had another modest set-back. Some lines of mine about the New Forest were shown (by Frank Young of Commins) to a publisher's traveller who—I understood—was also a sort of talent scout. Now we would certainly get somewhere, I thought! But he was obviously getting past his work: "I see nothing in these lines," he told Frank, "to lift them out of topography into poetry!"

And Sir Edward Marsh, the unhappy recipient of a confused mass of handwritten sonnets, replied that he couldn't conscientiously recommend me to go on. . . .

Traveller in Slates and Lime

I can't say at this late time why I got the sack from Hooper and Ashby's—and a thought strikes me: I have a sort of feeling I worked for them *before* I worked for Middletons! But no matter! I shall press straight on now to William Burgess (Ltd., no doubt; and afterwards Blanchard & Burgess, but I don't think I survived the amalgamation. The great shadowy boss in the background was Sydenhams of Poole, who had real ships tied up against their stockyards, and a private railway engine of their own going up and down the sidings. A proper crane, too, on the wharf.)

I had an interview with one of the heads, who called me Mr. throughout and spoke of "salary" when I had always thought in terms of wages. I was to be a traveller now and it was even thought (by me) that I would have a car.

But I learned that you can be a traveller on a bicycle; and you can supply your own bike, too. I got a maintenance allowance for my machine, I fancy—two shillings a week, was it?

I began with a local beat in Boscombe and Winton, gradually increased to take in Parkstone and Poole, but for some reason not Christchurch. As it became more and more apparent that very few of the builders in these areas were prepared to buy lime, chimney pots, timber (for I had added the timber trade to my list) and paints from me in any appreciable quantities I went further and further afield. By these means I extended still further my intricate knowledge of the by-ways.

Once a week I used to go to Blandford, taking my bike on the train; and from Blandford I used to cycle round to Okeford Fitzpaine and Sturminster Marshall and the various Winterbornes and so on. No go! I occasionally sold twopennorth of cement, or a few feet of seven-by-one country cut (pray excuse these highly technical terms) but taking the thing all round I cannot be called a success. From my own point of view there was little to be said for Blandford: no bookshop.

I again extended my beat, to take in Dorchester and Weymouth. I cannot honestly say that I recollect ever selling anything in either of these towns, but I want it clearly understood that I tried. I always made several calls before knocking off for the day to inspect the Roman remains, the Barnes statue, the great parish church of Fordington, and the other fine sights of Dorchester. As for Weymouth, I can bring witnesses that I called most persistently, pressing the merits of our slates and drain-pipes in the face of every opposition and to this day I attribute my non-success entirely to the fact that in those parts they have little use for supplies furnished from thirty miles distant when ships equally big tie up at the end of their own back-yards. With my own eyes I saw cement just like ours being unloaded at the quay next to what was practically a passenger liner due to sail for Jersey. What a grand place Weymouth was, I thought, sitting in the sunshine at the top of the Nothe and taking in on the one hand the fine panorama of Portland naval yard and on the other the bay and prospect of "the Naples of England"!

The world of Builder's Merchants is a comparatively restricted one. At Burgess's we had Pliny's brother working, and another link was forged with Holts when Nick Carter came to be a traveller. There was in fact, no vacancy for a traveller, and in order to accommodate Nick Carter one had to be created. . . .

And I don't think I have been to Okeford Fitzpaine or Sturminster Marshall since.

There are various ways of writing an autobiography. You can put in what will interest other people, and have a fairly short book, or you can put in what interests yourself and then learn that works of that kind went out with Augustus J. C. Hare. My final break with the trade of Builders' Merchant

came with the termination of my engagement with Burgess's—I
say final because it was eighteen years ago, and I don't suppose
any of my early employers would have me back now. The
designs (and the prices) of cleat hooks and rising butts have
altered enormously since my day. I'd have to begin at the
bottom again, and where would I be now with five shillings
a week?

But it does mean that I have next to recount a comparatively
dull stretch of my career, because look at it how you will
drawing the dole would figure ingloriously as the main content
of a chapter. I will leave these weeks of enforced idleness to
look after themselves and glance back over the nine years since
I had left school to glean whatever particulars may be added
those I have already told.

About 1931 I became eligible for the Rovers. I was the
only lad who had ever spent five years with the 13th Bournemouth (St. Peter's) Troop of Scouts without getting a single
badge. I was still a tenderfoot; or, if I did attain to Second-
Class Scout it was at the very end and doubtless in a sort
of honorary capacity. The reef knot I had mastered early
—"right over left, and turn; left over right, and turn" (or is that
a Granny?)—and I could pick up a clove hitch from the floor
with a dextrous turn of the wrist. But in such matters as saving
a drowning man, building a bridge with four scout poles and
grass, making a flap-jack over red-hot embers, or erecting a bell
tent in sixteen seconds starting . . . NOW! . . . I was useless.

But the Rover Scouts don't have badges for map-reading and
needlework and botany and splicing; all they have is a coloured
star for each year of service, and here time was on my side. I
put up five green stars my first day, to represent that long vista
of lost opportunities to shine in the Scouts as a basket-maker or
a signaller, and now and again I conscientiously added a
yellow one to them as 1931 succeeded to '32, '33 and the rest.
I honestly refrained from putting up any red Wolf Cub stars
although I had worn my brother's Wolf Cub cap and had even
gone courting in it, those years ago. And nobody would have

known, because by now Douglas was a soldier, in India; in fact, I believe he had gone even further and was a Mounted Policeman in New Zealand. He wasn't likely to find fault in my stars.

Winter scouting meant rather more reef-knot tying and P.T. than I cared for; and the parallel bars were a real purgatory, although it is true that when I joined the army my early scouting experience saved me from a few broken arms, etc. Because in the army even chaps who couldn't do "the scissors" and other fearful contortions had them to do and quite a number were carried off in various states of sprain, fit, concussion or simply bleeding to death. But as one of the Sgt.-Instructors said, what are soldiers for?

In summer, however, and, as we grew older, right round the year, we did a good deal of camping. Although we had several favourite spots our main camping headquarters was at Verwood, where the Rev. C. J. Hanson had a field behind the house, and a fine wooden bungalow attached to the house itself which could be used in winter and rough weather. Mr. Hanson moreover had the most exciting things inside the house—many, many books; a lathe; an electric pump for getting water from the well; a wireless transmitting licence and equipment which picked up all kinds of things ordinary sets never got a sniff of; wonderful cameras and developing machinery; a car in which we careered about the countryside with horn sounding non-stop and tyres screaming. And Mr. Hanson's conversation embraced most of the things we knew about, and amplified them. He it was who introduced us to *Stalky and Co.*, and Wilfrid Blunt's ballad beginning "I like the hunting of the hare", and Davidson's *A Runnable Stag*. Moreover, he knew lots of local magnates and when you were out with him you might meet a general or a bishop on almost equal terms. I'm not sure that we didn't once run one over, which gave us a momentary superiority.

Verwood is a large sprawling village in one of the less-known corners of Dorset—the top right-hand corner. Here are West Moors, Three Legged Cross, Horton, Edmonsham, Knowlton,

Cranborne and other fine places. Here are St. Giles, and Harley Gap, and South Damerham (that's in a funny little pocket of Hampshire) and within easy distance are Farnham Museum and Salisbury and Ringwood. Verwood is a brick-making district, with a sandy sub-soil and lots of pine woods and low, pine-crowned hills, and a good deal of open, rather marshy moorland. Here are those enchanted landscapes of my youth that I shall never see again but through alien eyes. Redman's Hill, Mount Ararat, Surprise Valley in Woodlands Park, Horton Tower and Horton Woods, Witchampton and Critchel and Sixpenny Handley! I made Redman's Hill the scene of one of those many love poems I wrote at eighteen and nineteen, when my understanding of this difficult subject was clear and precise, being founded on things read in books. The poem, here and there, is suspiciously like one by Robert Nichols, and lest anyone think he pinched from me I will at once confess that his poem to which I refer was published when I was three. So if there *was* any pinching it was on the other side His poem is called "Farewell to Place of Comfort" and is in *Ardours and Endurances* which adorned my shelves then, and still does.

I venture to quote my poem because in those days I couldn't understand why all the editors sent it back, and I promised myself that one day—despite them all—I would see the thing in print.

REDMAN'S HILL

Linger awhile, here on this twilight hill,
Hushed and remembering. Dear for our love's desire,
The pagan gods, the ancient deities,
Have fashioned now the magic of this night,
Knowing our sudden need. For this our love
Through all the bitter years has flamed and sighed,
Only for this. Dear, do not turn away,
I too am sad; for us, forgetfulness
Remains but in the arms you now forsake,
In traitor lips still ready to betray,
And in the mercy of the evening, sleep.

Here in the silence let us take farewell:
Our separate ways before us, desolate,
Dark with some dreaded mystery, shrouded lie.
Here let us pause. The weary years fall back,
My heart is filled with that first summer day,
Filled with your voice and tumbled wind-tossed hair,
And little whispered musicks torture me.

O tragic love! O promise unfulfilled!
Now I break faith with all I ever loved.
My prayers henceforth rise but as broken sighs,
Unfinished and unheard . . . those same strange gods
Heedless shall stand; love that has been my shield
Shattered remains—I dare not stoop to mend.

Ah mockery! Beauty I swore should live
Though I indeed might fail. O stricken dream!
See, darkness and no stars: night comfortless;
Let us return: cities, and men, and lights,
The new things call: the old, the best, the dear,
Sadly beloved, have failed us: this endures,
This petty second best that fools call life;
We who have lived may smile, who now are dead.

This hill of memory, O broken shrine! farewell.

I was particularly proud of that word "musicks" which I had
learned, I think, from A. C. Benson. I never found an opportunity to say "sate"—but I will!

Now for eighteen that poem isn't bad, but isn't it odd how
young men like broken hearts and shattered dreams and
death? I had not the smallest right to talk like that about
Redman's Hill. I had never sat on it in my life struggling with
an emotional crisis and sadly exchanging farewell kisses with
some fellow unfortunate whom fate had similarly blasted. We
used to go up and enjoy the view, and the only emotional
crisis I ever recall there was a heated argument about the
identity of a brickworks whose chimney we could see on the
horizon. Paul said it was at East Parley, which was absurd
because anyone could see it was somewhere by Ferndown—

i.e., about a mile further west. Farewell, broken shrine, you commanded a wide prospect and one day I must bring a girl on to your broad slopes and see what develops.

Generally speaking, however, I was not a topographical poet; the publishers' rep. had cured me of that. Love was my subject, and the sonnet its form. So:

> Wherein you bind me truly I confess
> I know and care not, but those bonds are bound
> Triple in strength, and me they do surround
> Precluding thought of exit or ingress.
> Yes, I'm encompassed so on every side
> I mayn't depart nor yet return again,
> But in my pleasure, ay! and in my pain
> In solitary confinement I abide.

> Till I loved you I thought of love no more
> Than now I think of freedom, but I thought
> Love was a game, for so I had been taught
> By those who claimed to know love's ways for sure.
> Go, little words, bring tidings to those same:
> What I've achieved of love is not a game.

I can't remember who inspired this one; about that time I had a number of girls with whom I thought myself in varying degrees of love—Doris, Ann, Margaret, Muriel, and one whose name escapes me. But I do remember the memorable experience of hearing this read aloud—declaimed, in fact—with magnificent effect by John Cowper Powys. How patient he was with my youthful importunities! How important he made me feel that I was, or at least, would be one day! Not many distinguished men of letters will knock off work for the day in order to recite the poems of an out-of-work ironmonger into their author's admiring ears.

But all this has seduced me away from Redman's Hill and Mr. Hanson with his field glasses, ready to observe the movements of a yellowhammer.

It was at Verwood that I learned all I ever did learn of philosophy, for Paul and Shindy would impart to Bob and me

the latest they had gleaned from the works of Bertrand Russell.
They were also able to keep us posted in the controversies
surrounding Bishop Barnes of Birmingham, who had no more
wholehearted supporter than Paul. Paul also knew all about
the stars and could point out Aldebaran and Sirius without fear
of contradiction. Shindy, who worked at the library, always
knew a little bit more about any author I might mention than I
did; which was vexing but had to be endured. Fortunately, he
never wrote poetry: or if he did, he kept quiet about it. Bob
lived an almost completely normal life in which the newest
speed records took precedence over both Bishop Barnes and the
rhyming dictionary.

Far into the night, in a hermetically sealed room about eight
feet square (and after all, it was December outside) we would
lie discussing God, girls, Bulldog Drummond, Bentleys and
Sir Henry Birkin and Hardy's *Two on a Tower*. One by one
we would fall asleep until the last thought he had secured an
unusually respectful silence and so found himself without an
audience.

Our principal activities were walking and cycling; but as
Shindy did not number cycling among his favourite pastimes
we tended more and more to walking. In those days "hiking"
was the newest word for this occupation, but we were careful
not to use it. Hikers were people of mixed sex in shorts and
open-neck shirts. We always wore long trousers and tweed
jackets and Paul never failed to affect a collar and tie. A
favourite means of passing a night was to take train to some
distant point—say, Brockenhurst—arriving an hour or so before
closing time. Supper at the local pub, and then a twenty-mile
walk home, taking the whole night for it, with pauses for
refreshment from a flask of boiling rum-and-coffee and even, if
there were a bright moon, a few hands of Solo. There are
comparatively few roads around Bournemouth that I have not
trodden in the small hours, discussing God, girls, and the other
subjects noted above.

By this time poetry—I mean the poetry of others, fortunately

6

published in books—was beginning to be my darling study. I found that it could be applied in ordinary life. "We have heard the chimes at midnight"—fancy anyone before us having been up and doing in the small hours! Again:

> . . . It is something to have done as we have done;
> It is something to have watched while all men slept,
> And seen the stars which never see the sun . . .

When I came across that bit of Chesterton I practically ran all the way to Paul with the news (I expect Shindy knew it already).

But in the lath-and-plaster business it is virtually no asset to be the author of more alleged sonnets than Keats, and the ability to quote Lascelles Abercrombie comes a bad second to quoting the latest price of laminated plaster board.

ITINERANT POET

In the early days when I used to get the sack it seemed plausible to blame my employers. They were, after all, but fallible men, more expert perhaps in putty and glass than in recognising exceptional possibilities in poetical apprentices. And I did keep my first job over four years.

But here and there it was now beginning to be thought that there might be faults on both sides. And there was another difficulty: Bournemouth did not furnish a limitless supply of Builders' Merchants. I had already been released from the pay-rolls of four of them. . . . The remaining three entered into no strong competition for my services.

I thought the time had come for me to be a writer, although I couldn't make up my mind yet what sort of a writer I would be. I had no intention of giving up poetry, of course, but I already knew that this was a branch of the trade in which the only reward was glory. In addition to being an important poet, I decided I must specialise in some commercially popular form. Perhaps the local paper would have me.

At this time the *Bournemouth Daily Echo* had a reporter whom I knew by sight. He used to come into the Cri., and could also be seen elsewhere about the town—following his occupation, I have no doubt, but to the uninstructed observer apparently enjoying a life of endless leisure. It was entirely my sort of life, that, I decided. Now one day I was walking up the slope of the cliffs above Branksome Chine when I encountered this reporter standing at the summit gazing out to sea.

"Excuse me, sir," I lost no time in beginning, "but I believe you are connected with the *Echo*?"

He said yes, he was. "I have been wondering if I might enter the profession," I continued, using the best prose style at my command. He asked me if I knew anything about it. No? Then there was very little hope. Moreover, it wasn't the sort of thing he would put *his* son into, personally. But I might read up a few books and then write to the editor. Certainly as he said all this he turned to me a face in which there was hope neither for me nor himself. And then he turned his sombre gaze back to the limitless sea. And I moved slowly on towards Canford Cliffs.

This was not encouraging, but I got the books and read in them. They taught me nothing, because I skipped the bits I didn't know, and the bits I did know (not many) I read with great attention and was thus able to persuade myself that all this elementary stuff was getting me nowhere. These pains-taking principles were framed for those who perforce had to begin at the bottom; but they could be by-passed by genius, luckily for me. However, my faith in the *Bournemouth Daily Echo* was shaken by the interview on the cliff, and I began to wonder if the provincial press offered sufficient scope. My talents ought first to be made available to the great national dailies, perhaps. London!—after all, I knew something of the metropolis, and a man who could find his way from Charing Cross Road to Bishopsgate, and who could take care of himself even in Glasshouse Street, was wasting his time in a place like Bournemouth.

London, however, was not my immediate goal. Rather than hang about out of work in Bournemouth I would be a tramp! I would shuffle along the lanes and support myself by selling my poems from door to door! My parents heard this declaration with proper scepticism and decided that the way to cure such foolishness was to acquiesce. All right, be a tramp then!

So I began to settle up my large affairs. I sold a good many of my books, retaining only so many as would go in the large glass-fronted bookcase that had been one of my twenty-first birthday presents. My mother paid my tailor's bill. I distributed various personal effects here and there: most of my maps to Paul, my Primus stove on long loan to Bob. I don't think my departure benefited Shindy materially, although he had once offered mé five shillings for the first edition of *Ardours and Endurances*. Neither by sale or gift did it come his way.

I presented—very grandly—a set of the works of Edgar Allen Poe to the library, and—very foolishly—a set of the *Biographia Britannica*. Those six fine quartos (or were they folios?) I have much regretted the lack of many times since, but a hint dropped once that perhaps they had only been loaned and ought now to be returned met with no acquiescence—very properly: for they were indeed a gift, and I hope the citizens of Bournemouth are queuing up to read them.

I cannot exactly recall what equipment I took for this adventure but my mother, mildly sarcastic, pointed out that tramps could hardly be permitted sheets and pillows. I took one blanket and a groundsheet to serve until I got accustomed to sleeping under old newspapers, and a rucksack that had once belonged to Pat Dear to carry my goods until I got accustomed to suspending them about my person with pieces of string. The night before I left, Shindy and I went round several remembered pubs and talked with increasing wisdom as the hours passed, of the things we had known. Shindy, I think, thought of me as one already dead. The rest of my acquaintances expected me home again with a cold in the head by the end of the week.

And so, on a Friday morning, I set up in business as a vagabond. My first feeling that the whole thing was a mistake came at the moment of departure, and I kept it to myself. I set forth boldly down the hill, turned left at the bottom into Vale Road, followed round into St. Clement's Road and over the bridge and so on, on, up the long pavements of Capston Road and into Winton. Here I was to meet my friend Mr. Burt the builder (he had been one of my best customers in the days when I was a traveller in nuts and bolts.) Mr. Burt had a big job on hand out beyond Shaftesbury, and he was going to give me a lift that far. After that my last link with civilization would be severed, for not only strange faces but strange scenes would surround me. My experience of the Dorset by-ways did not reach beyond the borders into Wiltshire; but I was aiming for the Midlands that are sodden and unkind—nor did I fail to quote Belloc to myself as I journeyed. Bidding Mr. Burt farewell I "cheered myself up with ends of verse and sayings of philosophers" (S. Butler, *Hudibras*) and "set my stumbling footsteps towards the light" (K. Hopkins, *unpublished.*)

Every now and then as I write this I pause to reassure myself. Have no fear, it will all come right in the end!—but was it really me to whom these odd things happened? I see that young man departing from Mr. Burt's building job towards the uncertain west sixteen years ago, thinner than I am now and without the moustache, but otherwise much the same, and I marvel. He might so easily have remained in Bourne-mouth and become at last manager of the wallpaper depart-ment. Or he might have frozen to death the first night under a hedge. Or, indeed, he might have gone on to be a famous poet, as he intended. But none of these things happened.

Certain bits of that journey remain vividly in my mind. My first independent enterprise was to buy a loaf of bread and a bit of cheese at Semley—I decided to put off begging for a day or two and get a bit more into the spirit of the thing. I had nearly thirty shillings in my pocket and I couldn't yet feel myself a genuine tramp: indeed, when I met one shuffling along I did my best to look like a hiker, and gave him a somewhat austere good-day. Time enough to learn the chalk-marks for "beware of the dog" when my pockets were empty. I sat at the roadside and ate my bread and cheese on a fallen tree, and while I sat there the farmer came along with another man and sold the tree for £3 and told me not to disturb myself—"Sir"—fancy calling a tramp, sir, I thought, nodding condescendingly.

On I went, past Sir Christopher Wren's birthplace at East Knoyle, until I got a lift for thirty miles or so, into Bristol. I didn't know quite what arrangements the city of Bristol made for tramps, so I put up at an hotel.

I had a friend in Bristol, Bill Dibben. He had been James Venn's partner in the Crescent Cottage Bookshop at Weymouth, where I had eaten so many huge Devonshire teas, and heard and seen many marvels. James Venn couldn't bear for me to pay for books, and if I bought one he always added two or three "on the house". Dibben was a bookseller in the same glorious tradition—and it is surprising how many of them there are. It is not a characteristic of most trades.

Dibben and Venn had contributed to make my first little book a financial success by taking about thirty shillings' worth. It was this pamphlet, or one like it, that I had a supply of in my knapsack, and it was designed to support me. If any of the three people to whom I sold copies on the road still have them they are possessed of a rarity: copies of that little work not signed by the author are almost unobtainable.

I will copy the description of it from an elaborate bibliography of the writings of Kenneth Hopkins which I began to keep a year or two later. This bibliography was in a quarto notebook large enough for listing the whole works of Balzac and it has since been used for more practical purposes. But it comes in handy now to furnish the following information:

SIX / SONNETS / by / Kenneth Hopkins / (device) / BOURNEMOUTH / Privately Printed / 1938.

100 copies printed in March, 1938. 8 pp., wire stitched in paper wrappers.

This work sold for a shilling, and I notice from the bibliography that it was my third book. *Twelve Poems* (1937) must have been the one so largely supported by Dibben and Venn; and *Recent Poetry* (1937) was apparently a sort of Christmas card, for I find it was published on December 25, in an edition of thirty-three copies.

As *Six Sonnets* was intended to keep me in bread, if not butter, I may be allowed to give a specimen here; but should I choose the best or the worst, I wonder?—for even so few sonnets as six can show great variations in merit, especially when I wrote them. Well, I have read them over—and have corrected a

mis-print which appears to have gone undetected since 1938—
and I have picked number three, for which, be it remembered,
the sum of tuppence would originally have been required.

SONNET

Love matched with time fights a defensive war,
Time seems love's most despoiler and dread foe,
But time delays its prescript, to prolong
Love's sweet swift moments, patient is time and strong
Being eternal, careless is time, being sure,
And kind in our long kisses, being slow.
Love makes a single war not of time's will
Which being warred against is peaceful still.

Our love makes truce with time, bids discord cease,
Throws down defence and hails the lapse of days;
Then time renews our love in many ways,
And our love's fear time lessens and allays;
Our love and tolerant time maintain this peace,
Whereby can love both prosper and increase.

"Sonnet? Pooh!" says the purist in prosody, "look at your
rhyme-scheme—if you can call it a rhyme-scheme!"

Now in 1944 I assisted at the birth of The Saturdays, that
society of poetry-lovers and writers, and many times have I
heard the subject canvassed. To some, only Petrarch may be
followed, with the rigid fall of rhymes afforded by his system; a
few admit the Shakespearean variation; and one or two more
will call anything a sonnet. Of these—obviously—am I.

I once inadvertently wrote a sonnet of only thirteen lines,
an accident which could never happen to the supporters of
Petrarch. Otherwise I have always followed convention by
taking the full fourteen; but in other ways I have been unkind
to the sonnet. I have written it in a sort of blank verse; I have
often used eleven, twelve or fourteen syllable lines, in among
the others, and now and then only nine syllables. I have
employed a great many different systems of rhyming—and
where has it got me? Ah!

At all events, on that chilly March night in 1938 it was one
of the factors that had got me to Bristol. I left my pack with

its concealed store of *Six Sonnets* at the hotel, and went forth to meet Dibben.

Excellent fellow! He took it for granted that the activities most of my Bournemouth friends thought mad were, in fact, perfectly natural. Indeed, one might almost have supposed that itinerant poets were passing through Bristol in a steady stream, each one receiving hospitality and encouragement from Dibben on the way. I don't think he thought much of my poetry, but he approved of my general outlook and policy; and, very important, he forced a pound note into my reluctant hand—which happened to be within his reach.

Dibben's various merits include the nicest taste in beer I ever encountered, and an appreciation of good sherry which ought to be numbered among the merits of every inhabitant of Bristol, but I suppose isn't; and if it were, precious little Bristol Milk would reach the outside world.

Somewhere in Bristol I had aunts and cousins, but this was no time for paying family visits, and anyhow I didn't know the address although I had once been there at the age of about four. So I spent the following morning inspecting the Cathedral, the fine and animated streets, the church of St. Mary Redcliffe —with a civil nod to T. Chatterton—and of course in visiting bookshops. At that time Mr. Douglas Cleverdon had a bookshop in Bristol and to him I sold a copy of *Six Sonnets*. From him I bought *Forty Poems* by W. H. Davies. It was Douglas Cleverdon who published one of T. F. Powys's stories with engravings by Eric Gill, and I was able to tell him what a choice item I thought it. I didn't add that for my copy no payment had passed, since it was one of several trifles inserted into my pocket one day unbeknownst before I left Crescent Cottage. No doubt any financial loss on that transaction was born by James Venn.

Leaving Bristol I made my way to Stroud where I had tea before pushing on towards Gloucester. It was dark and late long before I approached the city, and I decided to camp. Feeling a little ashamed of doing the thing in such style I unrolled my blanket and groundsheet, loosed a few buttons here and there, and lay me down in an abandoned barn, far from the haunts of men, and there abode. I slept tolerably, but woke stiff with frost and cramp about five, when it was getting light.

"Far from the haunts of men!"—not a bit of it. I had my head and shoulders in the abandoned barn all right, but my feet were practically inside someone's back door. It was a neat little house, one of a row pushed out into the country by the expanding industry of Gloucester. With infinite caution I buttoned up here and there, bundled my blanket and groundsheet back into the rucksack and crept slowly away, looking I suppose as furtive a figure as those parts had witnessed for a long time. Luckily only the parts, and not their inhabitants witnessed me. Once on the highroad I stepped out boldly for the city centre, feeling and looking like a tramp for the first time. I had breakfast and a sort of wash in the Lyons' teashop and pressed on to Warwick by lorry. From Warwick I walked and rode to Coventry (lunch) Birmingham, Wolverhampton, Shrewsbury, and on into Wales. My destination was Corwen.

Before reaching Corwen, however, I nearly got myself a job. One of the drivers who gave me a lift was seeking a cook for his yacht before setting out for Lisbon, and seemed impressed by the accounts I gave him of meals eaten at Mr. Hanson's. But of course I added that I had never actually held a badge for boy-scout cookery, and this admission may have counted against me. Anyway, he turned off into a side road before we had made any definite arrangement, and I got out and walked on to Chirk. My last ride was in the car with a man and two girls going to Llandudno, on the road which passes through Corwen, and in that small Welsh town they left me about ten o'clock. I had pushed a copy of *Six Sonnets* in among the cushions, and have often wondered whether it was ever found and commented upon. "But it must at least have been found," the reader cries. He has not fully understood that *Six Sonnets* was a *very* small book.

A Druid, a Disciple and an Ancient Mariner

"Corwen (Merioneth), M.8B, s.14, M.9B, s.14 Pop. 2,690 P. (Alt. 500 ft.)
M.D., *Frid.*; E.C., *Wed.*. [little drawing] *adj.* London 195."

I hope it is all right to quote from the *Michelin Guide* for 1926.
Such, then, was the township in which I now found myself.
Why had I chosen this resting place rather than one of a
thousand others up and down the land?

Because here lived John Cowper Powys.

I have had the good fortune to know a number of the great
writers of our time—the Powys brothers, Walter de la Mare,
Edmund Blunden, H. M. Tomlinson, Siegfried Sassoon . . .
—but to speak about them does not come within the purpose of
this book. I am now writing a light-hearted and superficial
record of my days and to say what these men have meant to me
would be to introduce a wholly different note. That is why I
have thus far not even mentioned my meetings and corres-
pondence with Llewelyn Powys and why I refer to them now
only to add that it was through him that I first met his brother,
John Cowper. That was in 1935, when J. C. P. was staying at
East Chaldon near his brothers. By 1938 he was established in
his house overlooking Corwen from the mountain slope, and it
seemed natural for my tramping to take me that way. Llewelyn
Powys I could not visit, for he was now living in Switzerland,
but I kept before me—though alas, I never sufficiently profited
by them—the wise words he wrote when he heard of my venture.
I fell, I think, always short of the ideal he would have had me
attain; but I believe I honestly aimed for it. It was an ideal
few of us ever reach, I suppose: something near akin to
Chaucer's perfect gentle knight.

What a wealth of good words have I heard in that little house up the mountain during my three or four visits to it! J. C. P. talks, I think, as S. T. C. must have talked. The range of his knowledge is immense, his enthusiasm is inexhaustible. How his eyes flash! He goes down, down, beyond the give and take of general conversation, leading his listener to the real truth of the matter. It is as though while the rest of us skim pleasantly across the sunlit sea he drops a lead right to the ultimate bottom—though it be five miles down—and to the anonymous monsters which he brings up, *he can give a name*. Old friend, I shall never find your fellow!—nor shall I ever justify the praise, never reluctant, or the confidence, never withheld, with which you greeted my poems and my plans.

Not far from Corwen lived another "formidable and terrifying genius"—James Hanley. These two households were in communication by telephone, though God knows the proper form would have been smoke signals or the unvarying tom-tom beat. If Corwen sheltered a Druid, the unsuspecting hamlet of Tynnant harboured an Ancient Mariner—and now I come to think of it, James Hanley *has* a strangely glittering eye!

So off I went to visit the Hanleys. Hanley, I felt, was a "real writer"—something I didn't specially associate with the Powys brothers, who were so much more to me than writers. They were Prophets at least, if not gods in their own right.

But James Hanley had a typewriter on the table with a half-finished page of manuscript in it, and a pile of completed pages lying at the side. He had a bookcase full of his own books, including *Boy* which had been banned. Lying about were various recent publications in which his stories and essays were printed—the *Left Review*, the *New Statesman* and the *London Mercury*. I had carried along with me my copy of *Men in Darkness* and this I now fetched out to be inscribed. It has a preface by J. C. Powys, and to this preface J. C. P. had already appended his signature. James Hanley now busied himself writing a long inscription on the fly-leaf, while I talked with

Mrs. Hanley, an occupation I was willing to follow for hours. I dare say *Six Sonnets* came in for its share of discussion.

It was arranged that I should spend the next night under the wide roof of Glan Cairw, and in the meantime James made use of my services in the garden digging up weeds before tea and my return to Corwen.

My two nights at Corwen were spent in the house of J. C. P.'s landlady, who was a local seer and told my fortune with remarkable fidelity; the things she told me that didn't, in the event, come true, ought to have done—e.g., that I would make money. To this fortune-telling talent she added a quite remarkable touch with bacon and eggs. But the next time I visited Corwen I stayed at the hotel, so as to be within easy reach of alcohol. That was about fifteen years later.

Having taken leave of J. C. P. and accepted ten shillings to see me on my way I left early in the afternoon for the Hanleys, upon whom I descended in time for a late lunch.

My visit to James Hanley confirmed my view that the best thing to be was a writer. Here was a man living in a fine house (almost a mansion) with plenty of books, pictures, flowers and other amenities. Just over the way was a wood full of primroses. He had a nice wife and an excellent small son. He could do gardening in the afternoon if he liked. He was hard up, he told me; and he was happy, as anyone could see. Tim Hanley asked me if I minded sleeping without sheets because the laundry hadn't come back. I was in no mood to mind anything. Hanley's autobiography, *Broken Water*, had come out not long since, and I was probably thinking of the day when I would write mine and record sleeping in his house without sheets.

In the morning I walked into the neighbouring village to buy stamps and one or two trifles of tobacco and the like for James. This was not the village of which he has since written so memorably in "Anatomy of Llangyllwch" (*Don Quixote Drowned*, 1953) and in other essays. But it was no doubt equally interesting to observe from the vantage point of Glan Cairw. The shopping for James took most of my loose cash and I was a little disconcerted when he paid me by cheque; that piece of paper would be of little immediate service during my long journey to London. However, not for the world would I have let on that the matter was of any moment; and I expect James hadn't tuppence in his pocket. I know more about writers now than I did then, and as I write this I have barely tuppence in my own. But I'll write anybody a cheque.

After lunch I began to retrace my steps—back to Corwen, back to Llangollen, back to Valle Crucis—this was off my route, but hadn't J. C. P. that very day in a five-minutes farewell chat told me that in his new romance he had reached a point where the hero (a youthful poet!) was at Valle Crucis Abbey? This information was enough for me! I lingered among the ancient ruins and wondered what sort of book this *Owen Glendower* would be. I didn't really approve of my Master writing historical novels: let his characters do it, if they liked. I wanted to read about people one might meet any day on Weymouth sands. But I readily made an exception when at last I came to read *Owen Glendower*, *Porius*, and *Atlantis*, for, as I ought to have expected, these were not like other historical novels.

I now began to get lifts in cars, lorries, even on motor cycles, and steadily moved towards London by way of Wrexham, Chester, Knutsford, Lichfield, Coventry . . . stopping at intervals for cups of tea in the busy cafes that serve the long-distance transport lorries and occasionally getting a fleeting glimpse of a cathedral, a castle, or a bookshop.

I enjoyed the chance companionship of these commercial travellers, lorry drivers and farmers who picked me up, carried me ten miles or a hundred, and then deposited me at some cross roads or corner. One chap advised me to get a job in the office-furniture business, and gave me several London addresses to apply at; I'm ashamed to say I never went near any of them. Another said some of the drivers carried a mate, and this information did interest me, but I never followed it up after all. I'd have enjoyed sitting in the cab of a twelve-ton lorry carrying sheet lead to Glasgow, or baking powder to Truro, or safety matches to Hull. But I suppose in the end I'd have got the sack.

Finally after all these various lifts I was picked up by a lorry on the Manchester-London service and brought in by St. Albans and Barnet to the North Circular Road, and dropped at Cricklewood. Here I got a bus for Marble Arch. It was seven o'clock on the morning of Thursday, April 14, 1938: Maundy Thursday. Hopkins was now a Londoner.

Living with Lenin

Both Llewelyn and John Cowper Powys had advised me to keep a diary. This advice, like so much that they gave me, I followed very imperfectly. But for about six months, beginning with my departure from Bournemouth, I did keep a record; that is why I am now able to say with such confidence that I arrived in London with two and eightpence ha'-penny (not counting Hanley's cheque, which though perfectly good represented capital not easily to be converted.) Somewhere in the post between Bournemouth and Corwen was a further ten shillings.

I had heard of Rowton Houses—had not W. H. Davies lived in one?—and I knew that down-and-outs slept on the Embankment, where they were awakened in the middle of the night by people with buckets of free tea. I expected to manage somehow, although at this first entry into the city I had no idea how to find a Rowton House or the river. It would have been absurd to worry about tonight's bed at seven in the morning. I got off my 16 bus at Marble Arch thinking more of breakfast than of the remoter future.

So I had breakfast in a small Lyons'—not the Corner House— and then to my great annoyance discovered that it had no place to wash. Now the Lyons' at Coventry and Birmingham both had towels and tablets of soap and hot water, all free, and I had never dreamed that London would lag behind the provinces in this way. I certainly wasn't going across to Hyde Park, where it cost tuppence to wash and you might get your pocket picked (true, there were meagre pickings in mine.) So I stayed dirty and telephoned Louis Wilkinson.

I had corresponded with Louis ever since J. C. Powys had

sent on to him several years earlier a poem of mine called *The Progress of Love* into which I had introduced as many words like bosom and thigh as I could think of. The poem was not altogether J. C. P.'s line of country, as he explained in one of those astonishing letters of his, but (poetry apart) Louis was entirely sympathetic. Here, once again, I had the luck to encounter a civilized and courteous spirit. Louis knew all about love.

My immediate need, however, was for a bath; but his telephone rang unanswered, and for the moment I had to abandon this part of my programme and go on to the next. "Don't fail to look up Charlie Lahr," Dibben had told me, able even from distant Bristol to direct and order my days. So I proceeded to look up Charlie Lahr; the only difficulty was that Dibben had said, "Red Lion Street, Hampstead"—or I had misheard him. And Hampstead does not boast a Red Lion Street, or a Charlie Lahr, as I learned after walking there from Marble Arch.

Oddly enough, this bookseller who was a household word in Bristol was entirely unknown on the edge of Parliament Hill Fields, which was my last point of enquiry. The best I could learn was that there were several Red Lion Streets dotted about the metropolis—this was before the completion of that wholesale change of names which obliterated so many famous thoroughfares: as if any right-thinking person wants to call Hart Street "Bloomsbury Way"! The nearest Red Lion Street was in Holborn and towards this I directed my steps, now flagging a little. All the same, I was safely on Charlie Lahr's doorstep—which he shared with the shop next door, and the three families living above—by ten. "If you're waiting for Charlie," said a complete stranger walking by, "he is never open before half past eleven."

Charlie Lahr has been described in a number of novels and autobiographies. One of the best accounts of him is in John Lindsey's *Vicarage Party*. (I was much impressed when John Lindsey came into Charlie's once and remarked that as he had no money he was going to take a taxi to his publishers and the man on the door would pay. How I longed to have a publisher with a man on the door, probably saluting me, and certainly ready to pay!)

But as a great many people must have read *Vicarage Party* and only three people have read my novel *Poor Heretic* (which remains unaccountably unpublished) I will quote the less familiar portrait given there. The hero, Christopher Adams (can you believe it?) is in a situation precisely similar to the one noted above in which I was placed. So we can go straight on without further explanation.

"Red Lion Street is ancient, it runs as it did perhaps four hundred years ago, straight down towards the old Foundling Hospital. Most of the grime of those centuries seems to have stuck to its old houses and shops. Some of the dust from surrounding districts may have blown in, too. Here and there one of the shops has its old eighteenth-century front window, behind whose misty panes can be seen broken china, tarnished brass, and all the accumulated rubbish of years in the old junk trade. It is a busy little street and at the bottom the clang of the trams in Theobalds Road joins with the roar of the buses at the top end, in High Holborn. Only at dead of night, when the noise of the local traffic has withdrawn, does a momentary peace fall upon Red Lion Street. The lights are all out except a few wall brackets jutting into the street here and there, and nobody much is about, but the cats and a policeman. You can hear the distant, all-night hum from Fleet Street and the Embankment.

"Christopher saw little of this at first. He saw a narrow street lined with shops and busy with constant traffic, and about fifty yards down an old hanging sign, 'Books'.

"The shop was closed. Its window was filled with the most unfortunate medley of unprepossessing books Christopher had ever seen. Besides being apparently the sweepings of the less cleanly jumble sales, these books had had time, here in the undisturbed seclusion of their final resting place, to acquire a coating of dirt more than sufficient to blot out their titles for

ever. Even as he gazed at them with some dismay, Christopher
saw a spider make its way across the back of what might have
been an odd volume of Paley's *Evidences*. Christopher wondered
what manner of man it was who kept this interesting shop.
Just then the man appeared, riding a bicycle.

"As the door was being unlocked Christopher introduced
himself as a friend of Dollery's, at Bristol. Mr. Lear knew
Dollery well. Christopher began looking at the books as the
shopkeeper put his stalls out. Christopher saw that on these
stalls were books certainly dirtier and probably duller than any
in the window. He guessed that those in the window were
serving an apprenticeship and would presently be promoted to
the busy life of the stall. If one book were sold from here in a
month, Christopher thought, it would be a miracle.

"Mr. Lear apparently did not deal in new books, but he
seemed to have an extensive practice in the sale of magazines
and papers. Most of these papers Christopher had never heard
of. They included *Forward*, *Moscow News*, *New Leader*, *Controversy*, *Tribune*, *Labour Monthly*, *Socialist Vanguard*, and a bright
red cover which proclaimed *The Right Review*. It appeared to
be blushing in this company.

"Mr. Lear, who had been running in and out of the shop as
though it were necessary for him to get his stalls arranged
outside in record time now came in to stay. Taking no notice of
Christopher he seated himself in the darkest corner of the shop
and began to read *The Daily Worker*.

"Christopher went on looking about him. The shop was
about ten feet by twelve, and the front wall was all window.
The door was at the side opening not into the street but into the
passage. As the window was lined floor to ceiling with books,
and had also a screen at the back, practically no light penetrated into the shop. The walls were lined with books, and in
the middle was a gas radiator over which a rickety arrangement of shelves supported, precariously, great piles of periodicals,
books, pamphlets, a typewriter, string, about two thirds of a
loaf, several pipes and various oddments of indiarubber, cheese,

carbon paper, matches and pipe dottles. These last were close to the radiator, drying for future consumption.

"With one thing and another occupying the floor space, little remained save a rectangular area with a slight depression at the back in which Mr. Lear's chair was established. The clear space was a bit larger than the top of a dining table, and provided standing space for about four people at a time.

"On the screen backing the window were a quantity of newspaper cuttings, some photographs, a number of brightly-coloured but rather crude surrealist drawings, a few obscene remarks inscribed in pencil, a great many telephone numbers and similar memoranda—including several customers' ledger accounts, apparently—and a bunch of newspaper contents bills bearing impossible legends: 'Hitler Punches the Pope', 'Mussolini 100 not out', 'Mr. Chamberlain on "The Hollywood I Love" ' and 'Stalin Kisses Trotsky'. These had some appearance of being home-made.

"Christopher's survey had now reached the proprietor of this remarkable establishment.

"Charles Lear was a man of about fifty, with greying hair brushed straight back. His moustache and goatee beard were of a faded ginger hue. His rather gaunt face appeared to have met all weathers, and now it had taken the colour and almost the texture of old leather. Mr. Lear found it convenient to wear a shirt of bright orange, and as his trousers were grey and his coat blue Christopher thought himself justified in supposing the socks would be green; but there were no socks. Mr. Lear's feet were contained in sandals. They were large and clean, and funnily enough they didn't look cold.

" 'Is there anybody you know about here who'd let me have a room for a night or two?' asked Christopher. 'I'm in a bit of a hole until I get some money from home. I'm expecting a letter at Edward Raynes', but when I rang him up he wasn't in. I've just got here from Manchester.'

"Mr. Lear, who knew everyone, knew Raynes.

" 'Ring him again,' he said, nodding towards a telephone under a pile of books.

"Still no answer. 'That means I shan't get my money today, I'm afraid,' said Christopher. But Mr. Lear had vanished.

"Now Christopher heard him calling from upstairs.

"On the first floor Christopher found him in a little room about eight feet by six, containing a bed, a small fireplace with a gas-fire and ring, an old armchair, a cupboard, a small table, and about a thousand books on shelves round the walls. Little space remained for Christopher to go in, unless Mr. Lear came out.

" 'You can stay here, if you like,' said the bookseller.

" 'This will do fine! How long can I stay?'

" 'As long as you like.'

" 'What's it worth?'

" 'Five shillings a week?'

" 'Can you wait a day or two?'

" 'Of course. Why not?' "

So that was settled and I moved in. Charles produced a kettle, a tea-pot, a cup, and other things. I unpacked my knife and fork, set my books in a vacant few inches of shelf, and began to feel at home. Charles had given me two keys, one to the street door and one to the room.

Now at last I had my overdue wash—at the tap in the cellar. I combed my hair, too. Then I went out shopping to lay in stocks for the long week-end before me. According to *Poor Heretic*, which is the authority for this period in my life, Charles pressed three shillings upon me before going home that afternoon. Of this I have no direct recollection, although it is exactly the sort of thing Charles would have done. Perhaps he cashed Hanley's cheque; he certainly knew Hanley and told me a long and complicated story about Hanley's teeth. But whatever happened even the remnants of my two and eight would have gone a good way in those days. I bought bread, cheese, tea and sugar and milk, and butter and jam. These, with fresh fruit, were my staple diet for the next eighteen months.

Back in the room I put the kettle on and proceeded to eat most of the groceries I had brought in. I was excited and happy, and so far I had had no time to feel lonely. The street was quieter now, people were going home. Tomorrow was Good Friday.

Looking now more closely at my lodgings I discovered that I was under the slightly mocking eyes of a portrait of Lenin. This head-and-shoulders drawing was life-size, or perhaps a trifle larger. It was impossible to ignore it, once aware of its presence, and when I lit the gas Lenin appeared to be floodlighted, for whereas the books absorbed the light, Lenin reflected it.

After a few weeks we became inseparable.

Poet up One Pair of Stairs

That first week-end in London set the pattern for my week-ends for a long time to come. After tea, lingered over but finished at last, I went out to occupy the city I had inherited. Very few inhabitants remained now, and I thought particularly of the thousands on their way to spend Easter at Bournemouth. They could have it!

What I specially revelled in was the anonyminity of London. If I cared to shuffle along in the gutter with my shoulders hunched and pick up fag ends, there was none in all that vast city to comment or condemn. I never actually picked up fag ends myself, but I watched with great interest those who did. I thought they smoked them—but nothing of the kind. An ancient wayfarer sitting under Hungerford Bridge by the old Lion Brewery once put me right on this point. He had a pile of tobacco about two feet high before him, and he was peeling the paper off his stock of fag ends and adding the contents to the pile. I forget how much a pound he said he could get for the stuff, but apparently he did a good trade with the dingy back-street shops that sell "Buzz-Fuzz Mixture: Our Own Blend, Try It."

But if I didn't pick up fag ends, at least I shuffled. I liked to think of myself as the poet Hopkins starving in London, and I'd go along the Embankment composing an imaginary biography. "At this time Hopkins was living in the depths of penury and squalor. The girl Mimi had deserted him for opium and the needle. Behind the dingy façade of the house in Red Lion Street he wrote far into the night, fashioning sonnets that were to be the despair and glory of the nation that had scorned him"—etc.

Meanwhile, Mimi having not yet appeared—alas, nor did she ever—I awakened on Good Friday to my breakfast of bread and jam and set myself thereafter in earnest to explore the city.

Everything was a delight. Even the enamelled plates bearing the names of the streets were an enchantment, with their legends, familiar or queer, now Chancery Lane, now Leather Lane, now Newgate Street, now Cheapside. All these were like old friends. And the narrow alleys, the courts between the buildings with glimpses of green trees among the cliffs of brick and stone, and here and there a church with its tower coming level with the shoulders of the banks and insurance offices around. At last I came on to the wide level of London Bridge, and naturally I murmured to myself, "London Bridge is broken down!"

This was my first sight of London River—as I was careful to call it, for was not this The Pool lying silent below me? A couple of ships lay at the south side under the sloping cranes, but Adelaide Wharf was deserted. In mid-river lay row upon row of barges, black and red, some empty, a few stacked with timber. I stood long looking at the many-pointed skyline, thinking of the company that had seen and loved it before me— poor men and thieves, many of them, men of a proud and angry dust, young and intolerant, old and embittered, men like Greene, like Otway, like Savage, like bright, broken Maginn, like James Thomson, Gissing, Middleton, Butler. These were the men I fancied standing beside me, looking at the water, watching the shadows changing, watching the pigeons and gulls.

It is a good way to look at London. Johnson and Lamb and Dickens are not the only worthies to be tracked down. I went once on a house-to-house scrutiny of Blackfriars Road to discover the place where Richard Middleton had lived— Charles put me on to him. When I began to write short stories Charles used to come along with armsful of books—"He's good!"—"Do you know her?"—"Ever read this?" until I felt that it would be a crime to add any more stories to the pile. It was a crime I hastened to commit.

But that came later. Meanwhile, it is still Good Friday—the

longest Good Friday I ever passed, I think. After returning to
my room for bread and cheese I went off in the other direction
and found Covent Garden, deserted and sweet smelling and
silent. All the best things in London I discovered for myself in
this way, often after plodding through miles of unrewarding
streets. That's why I feel a proprietorial right in the tomb-stone
of Mrs. Aphra Behn, in the tiny sundial-court off St. James's
Street, in Ely Place, in Clerkenwell Green, in Paddington
Basin, in South Audley Street Chapel and St. Bartholomew
the Great and Smithfield and in the camels that hold up the
Embankment seats.

My diary entry for the following day begins, "I have $\frac{1}{4}d$. in the
world. I have half a small loaf, some sugar, about enough
butter to spread one slice, and an Oxo." This diary is as
interesting a document in its way as the aforementioned novel
which no one would publish. The strange thing to me, looking
now over the faint pencilled entries, is where the money went.
"2s. from Paul," I record on one page, and a few lines lower
down, "I have $1\frac{1}{4}d$. Christ! I wish Ann were here," etc., etc.
I always seemed to have money to buy books: "Bought *Fool's
Quarter Day* for 8d. and L.U.W. signed it," or, "*Sugar in the Air*
(good book) 6d."

Here is a cash account which I kept for about two weeks soon
after I began to get the dole. It will be seen that I lived in
comparative comfort on that seventeen shillings a week. The
account is not in strict book-keeping tradition, but I will
reproduce it as it stands. I suppose nobody now will insist upon
its being audited.

MONDAY, 12th Sept., 1938

		s.	d.	s.	d.
Cr.	Cash in hand		$9\frac{3}{4}$		
Dt.	Milk				$1\frac{3}{4}$
	Stamp				$1\frac{1}{2}$
	Tube				1
	Bread				4
Cr.	Advance from Betty		6		
Dt.	Tube				3

Tuesday, 13th

		s.	d.	s.	d.
Dt.	Milk ($\frac{1}{4}$d. extra for carton)				2
	Sugar				$2\frac{1}{4}$
Cr.	Borrowed from Chas.	1	0		
	Received from Boyne Grainger		4		
Dt.	Beer (entertainment)				5

Wednesday 14th

Dt.	Milk				$1\frac{3}{4}$
	Tomatoes				$2\frac{1}{2}$
	Newspaper				1
	Butter				$1\frac{3}{4}$

Thursday, 15th

Cr.	Received from Chas.		$6\frac{1}{2}$		
Dt.	Milk				$1\frac{3}{4}$
	Bread				$2\frac{1}{2}$
	Cheese				3
	Butter				2

| | | 3 | $2\frac{1}{4}$ | 3 | $0\frac{3}{4}$ |

(This was a short week because the account began on a Monday.)

I will now give a complete week's budget. It will be noticed that I lived on the best of everything—best butter (2 oz., $1\frac{3}{4}d$.) and as much bread as I could eat. "Beer 5d." was a pint of mild.

Friday, 16th Sept.

		s.	d.	s.	d.
Cr.	Dole	17	0		
	Balance bt. forward		2		
	Profit on book sold		3		
Dt.	Tube				1
	Milk				$3\frac{1}{2}$
	Cakes				2
	Bread				$3\frac{1}{4}$
	Butter				$3\frac{1}{2}$
	Rent			5	0
	Owing to Chas.			1	$6\frac{1}{2}$
	Sugar				$2\frac{1}{4}$
	Stamp				$1\frac{1}{2}$
	Birthday cards and stamps				$5\frac{1}{2}$
	Book (*Mr. Norris Changes Trains*)				3

SATURDAY, 17th Sept.

		s.	d.	s.	d.
Dt.	Milk				1¼
	Bread				4
	Cakes				3
	Tomatoes				2
	Bath				6
	Gas				4
	Laundry			1	9½
	Tube Fares (entertaining guest)				2
	Bus Fares (entertaining guest)				2

SUNDAY 18th

		s.	d.
Dt.	Stamps		3
	Bus		2
	Tube		1
	Beer		2½
	Milk		3½
	Tube		3
	Tube		3
	Tram		6
	Gas		1

MONDAY

		s.	d.	s.	d.
Dt.	Cheese				3
	Fruit				2
	Envelopes				3
	Tube				1
	Tube				1
	Book (*On Education*, Russell)				1
Cr.	Profit, book (*On Education*) sold to Chas.		3		
Dt.	Milk				1¾
	Stamp				1½
	Bus (entertainment)				2
	Beer				2½
	Book (T.F.P. *Soliloquies*)				6

TUESDAY

		s.	d.	s.	d.
Dt.	Butter				3½
	Sugar				2¼
Cr.	Loan from Chas.		6		
Dt.	Potatoes				1
	Dripping				1½
	Bread				2¼

WEDNESDAY

		s.	d.	s.	d.
Dt.	Milk				1¾
	THURSDAY				
Cr.	Recovered from Alan		6		
Dt.	Milk				1¾
	Bread				3
	Milk				1¾
	Cinema				6
Cr.	Of Chas.	1	0		
Dt.	Telephones				3
		19	8	19	0¾

In this week I must have had at least one hot meal—for I cannot remember ever eating potatoes raw. Perhaps I boiled them in milk the day I had that extra half pint, and then stirred in melted cheese and beer—though I hope not.

This cash account has somewhat seduced me from the main story; for whereas (as demonstrated above) by September I was handling nearly a pound a week, at Easter I was sitting with a farthing in my pocket saying Christ!—which I was not to be blamed for. I must now retrace my steps and show how my fortunes changed so markedly for the better.

A fair sprinkling of the customers (a courtesy term) who used Charlie's shop as a club were either on the dole or about to be and thus I had at my command the best of advice. On the Tuesday after Easter I went to sign on; and in due course I received not only a weeks' money for the current week, but arrears from the time I left Bournemouth which amounted to about thirty shillings. That fixed me up financially though I am bound to confess the whole business was very inconvenient. I had to report for duty three times a week at the Labour Exchange off Pentonville Road—and that was no mean journey from Red Lion Street. The annoying thing was that a friend of mine in Sandland Street, a few doors from Charlie's, was able to report at Snow Hill, which was a bare five minutes' walk for him. The whole business of area boundaries needed looking into, I told the people at Pentonville. But they took no notice. It used to cost me about sixpence a week in fares to collect their miserable pittance.

A bit later on, during the war, another friend of mine *had the money brought to him* (so he said) because he told the Manager seventeen shillings wasn't worth going to collect in bad weather. But my friend had a black beard, and a cultured manner, which made a difference. Once you get a half-starved look, like I had, they kick you around something dreadful.

An assured income at sixty, the advertisements say. Pooh! I had one at twenty-two.

My next step was to get a ticket for the British Museum Reading Room, and this I accomplished without any difficulty, backed by the powerful name of John Cowper Powys—and was I not myself already represented in the Catalogue by a Work— *Twelve Poems*. That alone, I told myself without an atom of truth, would open every door.

I was now not only a poet, but a Scholar. I could speak of incunabula with the easy familiarity of complete ignorance, and never be challenged except by the comparatively restricted company of my fellow ticket-holders: for to every protest, could I not reply, "It's in the B.M., and *I've seen it!*"

I announced to a respectful audience (Charles, F. A. Ridley, Alec Bristow) that I had commenced a life of John Donne. There was good reason for this. Some time ago, Harold Pepin of the Bournemouth Public Library had detected in my works an affinity with those of Donne (which I had never read) and when I examined the Songs and Sonnets, the Elegies, and the rest, I detected it too. Naturally, the seventeenth-century poet laboured under disadvantages—an uncouth language, a defective ear, and whatever else must hinder one who has not received an elementary school education. Still, I could see that in his way he had occasionally anticipated me. With a generosity therefore as rare as it was misplaced, I decided to put him on the map. I would write the fellow's life; and although in fairness to myself I would have to tell people that my poems had been written *before* I read his and that any chance affinities therefore were congenital, I would gracefully concede that there was even less chance that he had derived any instruction from my writings.

And, lest it surprise you to learn that I had become a metaphysical poet so soon after the uncomplicated heart-cry of *Redman's Hill* I must tell you that we poets often command more than one string to our lyre. The following is certainly metaphysical enough for anybody:

HIS FAREWELL TO METAPHYSICK

You've wrung from me five drops of my thought's blood,
And mingled with your own thought's brilliant flood,
Wherein they lose my thought's identity.
Come; you must make your settlement with me.

You'll say, Not thus. You'll say, By these strange means
Little's accomplished for your spirit's good,
But I'll repay as any lover would,
In kind, and kindness shewn to you, you'll say.

Now let me put this surmising away;
Henceforth when I devise my woven rhyme
I will discount what seems the harder way,
I'll credit you with understanding this
Without more tidings of it, and I'll write
What's true and commonplace and dull and trite.

I'll never more so intricately spin
My twisted rhyme-scheme in and out and in
To follow difficult rhythms of my thought
Whose pale blood's best your delving cup has caught,
Till bonded thus in words of curious skill
Their later meaning is more difficult still
When all that needs to pass between us is
Settled, complete, accomplished in a kiss.

The resemblance to Donne is perhaps not everywhere apparent; but I didn't know that then. I was in the position of the man in *Hudibras*:

He knows what's what, and that's as high
As metaphysic wit can fly!

Several of the people who came into the shop unsuspectingly bought *Six Sonnets*, especially after R. B. Marriott reviewed the book in *The Era*. I cannot think what the regular readers of that excellent paper (now like many good things, no more) made of the information that here was a poet (i.e., me), new and significant, whose book was a rare bargain at a shilling. Nor was this the sum of Marriott's civility, for in due course he took time off from the office to be a witness at my wedding.

Unfinishing The Life of Donne

Not only did Charles know everybody, but everybody knew Charles, which is quite another thing. Consequently, apart from the regulars, the shop was always being visited by people I had heard of from afar and could now marvel on at close quarters. Here for the first time I saw Anna Wickham, H. E. Bates, Rhys Davies, Ronald Duncan, Julian Symons, Walter Allen, A. J. A. Symons, Leslie Halward, C. H. Norman, Philip Lindsay, Rupert Croft-Cooke, Malachi Whittaker, Gay Taylor, Gerald Kersh, Hamish MacLaren, E. W. Martin, Oswell Blakeston, A. S. J. Tessimond, L. A. Pavey, Charles Duff, Jack Mc-Laren, and many others. Some of these subsequently became my friends, others in the rush and clamour probably didn't even catch my name. For Charles's shop was like a mad house from about twelve till three.

I have said the floor space was restricted; perhaps four people could stand inside the shop in reasonable comfort, without jostling one another. But reasonable comfort was nothing to Charles's customers, and jostling to them was second nature. A typical day would find F. A. Ridley, Ernest George, A. B. Mace, Count Potocki, Charles himself (energetically saying, "Christ! Get out of my shop, can't you!") Alec Bristow, Oswell Blakeston in that vast camel hair coat, me taking in as much as I could, John Boylan, Frank Grainger, Arthur Downes, and a few late-comers shouting on the pavement. What few coherent scraps of conversation could be heard in the general din might have been something like this:

"My book on the Jesuits conclusively demonstrates . . ."

"Marx never maintained any such thing . . ."

"She ranks as our Mistress and takes precedence as our Countess . . ."

"Chamberlain, politically discredited, intellectually impotent . . ."

"I'm a bit of 'umanity and so are we all . . ."

"Stalin knows, none better . . ."

"All right, I said, so I turned her upsidedown and . . ."

I was sorry I missed that last bit.

Few of these regulars ever bought anything; most of them were content to read *The Daily Worker*, *Socialist Vanguard*, *Forward*, etc., from the piles of Charlie's stock, and if this proved impossible they would say casually, "Charlie, I'll just borrow *Moscow News* until tomorrow" and stuff it into their pocket. To almost every direct observation addressed to him Charles replied, "Christ!" or, "What's the good?" "Bastards," he would say, "they steal my books, borrow my papers, clutter up my shop, use my telephone . . ." and muttering imprecations he would spread out two or three old newspaper bills and set to work with paste and scissors to produce something like: "HORE BELISHA BLACKS CHORUS GIRL'S EYE" or, "BALDWIN CITED BY PIER" (this was too complicated for me.) Charles would also disappear every now and again to hang tickets, "Sacrifice. £5", on the backs of cars in the street. "I'll teach them to park outside my bloody shop, bastards!"

We had a novel way of making a quarter of tea do the work of eight ounces. I would make and drink tea in the usual way, dishing out cups to favoured customers like Malachi Whittaker, and an hour or two later Charles would fill up the pot to the top with water (sometimes boiling and sometimes not) and proceed to drink a pint or two of the result.[1] His diet generally was less luxurious than mine. Bread, certainly, a piece of cold sausage occasionally and once, I think, a banana, skin and all.

These people were all extraordinarily kind to me. Alec Bristow took away my silly plays and conscientiously read them and gave me advice about getting work with the B.B.C. and

[1] This practice has the authority of *The Rasciad*.

Radio Normandy. L. A. Pavey set me at writing stories and took them to Curtis Brown the literary agent and told me not to have plots with too many bosoms. Rupert Croft-Cooke told me how to get into magazines I had never heard of, which none-the-less paid good money, and encouraged me with the information that he wrote six novels before selling one. Anna Wickham told me not to let failure deter me: "Everybody fails that's any good!" And Malachi Whittaker never for a moment accepted a lower estimate of my merits than my own! When the Golden Cockerel Press wrote that my *Progress of Love* was unprintable, even in a strictly limited edition, and especially if it were intended to be illustrated, I felt I was indeed making headway.

My chief crony in those days was F. A. Ridley. He lived over the way almost within hailing distance, and we used to set forth most nights to walk to the Park, discoursing at large and with me carrying, disciple-like, the little stool upon which presently Ridley would mount to harangue the mob. I came to know every yard of the way from Red Lion Street to Marble Arch. We used to cut through the back streets—probably going by way of Bedford Square, New Cavendish Street, and Portman Square, and returning, perhaps, by Grosvenor Square, Great Marlborough Street and High Holborn. "Hopkins!" Ridley would say, "you are a man of parts. I will go further: you are a man of genius!" "I know it," I would reply.

In the Park, Ridley would set up his stool and I would stand below and he would begin.

"The way to collect a crowd, Hopkins," he would say in a low, confidential tone, "is to speak so quietly that they can't hear you. So they come in a little nearer, by ones and twos, being curious, and the ones and twos behind press in upon those in front and before you know where you are you can begin to speak louder and say THIS EVENING I AM GOING TO TELL YOU SOMETHING YOU DIDN'T KNOW ABOUT DIALECTICAL MATERIALISM! MY FRIENDS . . ." It was then safe for me to slip away and hear what Bonar Thompson was up to, or to go along to the

No-Godites pitch and puzzle over the weekly question, "All right. So God can do ANYthing. Perhaps the questioner will tell me how God can make a bell ring less than once?"

"*Jesus loves me, this I know*," the singers would wail.

"As my friend Mr. Ramsay MacDonald will tell you . . ."

"What is Poetry, you ask? Sir, read my works and you will find the answer . . ."

"And oo pays for it? The Government? The State? Some philanthropist perhaps? No, my friends: it is paid for by you!"

One day, to my sudden shame and confusion, Ridley announced in a loud voice, "I have in my audience tonight the greatest living poet!" "Where's the poet?" said three voices. "Show him! Show him!" I blushed and slunk away.

When Ridley was not confounding the hosts of Heaven in Hyde Park he was demonstrating the force of reason as exemplified in the teachings of Prince Kropotkin and others of whom also I had never heard, on Tower Hill. "It's a tough audience on Tower Hill," he would affirm, "but I collected enough money there one morning to get married!"

After looking at his hearers with great scorn he would begin, "ALL RIGHT, so you've got jobs and money in your pockets and a week's holiday with pay! You're not the sort to be exploited, to be downtrodden, to be gulled. You know the Tory measure, you can meet it!" (leaning forward, suddenly confidential) "Listen, my friends . . ."

But I would wander away into the magical streets, among the ships and cranes and churches and the smells of tar and spice. . . . "Could I escape unrest," I wrote in the only poem I ever had printed three times, "it would be here . . ."

> Could I escape unrest it would be here
> Where the city meets the river by St. Paul's,
> Where small strange courts between the grimy walls
> And crooked passages with names antique and queer
> Lie quite unvisited except by little birds
> And sound of chiming bells that name the lapsing hours,
> By river sounds, and far-off shouted words,
> And by the changing shadows of tall towers.

> Here by the bridge I'd not remember care
> That cankers the world's heart and lurks in mine,
> But I'd put off my troubles, like a cloak
> From sun-warmed shoulders, leaving them quite bare;
> So all my heavy thoughts I would resign
> And watch the swirling tide and drifting smoke.

And in another poem which I began and forgot to finish I said:

> I will walk in London with a girl beside me,
> Through the Middle Temple to the Thames we'll go.

And so we did. One morning when Charles called in with a letter for me there was a squeak and a scurry under the bed-clothes and I had to explain that I was entertaining a visitor— as a big-toe sticking out at the bottom of the bed confirmed: for I happened to be standing four-square on the floor. Too much walking by the Thames had made the lady regrettably miss what I assured her was the last train to Bournemouth.

About half past twelve each week-day I would stroll round to the Museum, often accompanied by Ridley. My day was made if, just as I passed into the Reading Room with a lordly air, some wretched provincial was turned away by the door man saying in a hushed voice, "Readers Only!" "Back to the Elgin Marbles, dog!" I would mutter. I was a Reader—and a Writer too, by God. Not every Reader, I can tell you, can be found in the Catalogue under HOP.

Securely settled at seat N.6 or the nearest to it if by some mischance a stranger had taken that one, I would read the works of Aston Cokain and Petherik Jenkyn and Edmund Prestwich and Samuel Pick and occasionally add to my own. "Wrote Seven Sonnets in 1¾ hours at the B.M.", my diary notes. "That's quarter of an hour each!" Well, so it was; I was now not only writing more sonnets than Keats, but writing them faster.

My evenings were pretty well occupied, too. Sometimes I would go off to Louis Wilkinson's for supper and a bath, and sometimes to two girls who lived at Pimlico and afforded the same facilities with the kindness I was beginning to think common to all Londoners. In their flat looking across to the flood-lighted Battersea Power Station I first saw a print of Van Gogh's "Sunflowers". I had no idea anyone painted like that but apparently *he* did; and they told me there were a lot of modern paintings in the Tate Gallery, nearby. Luckily at this time I was not also confronted with Chagall. But I did—with a very knowing air—patronise a set of canvasses by Braque in the gallery at Brussels a year or two later. You were safe, I had learned, if you said little and wore your head slightly on one side.

Louis Wilkinson had a flat in Albion Street, Lancaster Gate, and was much put out about this time because they changed the name to Barrie Street. He didn't hold with Barrie. Louis lived right at the top of a high house—the flat is described in his novel *The Devil in Crystal* (by "Louis Marlow")—and he used to give careful directions to callers. "Ring the top bell and then go out into the road and I will throw down the key to you," he would counsel. An old glove would come hurtling down, with Louis leaning out dizzily from a vast height to watch the place of its fall. Occasionally it would bounce into the basement area and have to be fished out again with infinite care.

Inside, Louis had just what I longed to have: two big rooms full of books and pictures and old furniture; a vast bed—"It easily holds three" he told me, as one who knew; an oil painting of a lady without any clothes; a kitchen and bathroom with constant hot water; *Pills to Purge Melancholy*; and a view through a gap in the houses of the Long Water in Kensington Gardens. Mercifully, he was denied the sight of Peter Pan.

As for Louis himself! what could I add to the self-portrait in *Swan's Milk* and *Forth, Beast!*—except that he was my first contact outside of books with the manners and outlook of the eighteenth century.

Another, and very different port of call, was George Padmore's. George was living then near Victoria, and Ridley and I used to tread through the darkened streets and squares until we came to the little gate that led down to a basement almost completely under the road. Here were excellent talk and cups of tea and the chance of hearing Chris Jones, or Jomo Kenyatta. These men I knew only slightly, but George Padmore's gentle friendship I enjoyed and valued from the first. Chris Jones I know would have proved such another, but for his tragic and early death. I rode in a tram with him one evening along the Embankment and for once never looked at the lights and the moving waters; for Chris in his quiet voice was telling me something of Africa.

Then there was the flat in Lamb's Conduit Street where Count Potocki was established with his printing press and his claim to the kingdom of Poland.

I am not competent to decide upon the merits of this claim. I was perfectly willing to accept it as reasonable from so charming a host, and then and now I wished him every success in it. Poland might do worse than try another monarchy, I reflected, as I climbed the forty-odd stairs to this royal abode. Count Potocki occasionally printed my poems in the *Right Review*, and poets like to get their work printed. It was all very fine for Ridley to tell me that the poets' salvation lay in socialism, if none of my poems could get into the *Left Review*. And didn't Potocki once introduce me, *as a poet*, to the Earl of Mar!

So I drifted along through the summer of 1938, talking, arguing, walking, exploring; learning, too. My parents were satisfied that I was in no immediate danger from the white slave traffic and other perils; in fact they rather liked Charlie Lahr and when they sent me a food parcel Charles used to get a share.

The only thing that didn't prosper was my life of Donne. Donne, I discovered, had a dullish life; his wild youth is singularly ill documented; his sedate maturity I was unable to find of interest. And anyway he was the subject of a biography by Isaac Walton.

Had anyone, I wondered, ever written a life of Isaac Walton? Yes, even that had not been overlooked.

Alas, Working Again

Twice in my life the Labour Exchange has upset all my plans by sending me after a job. And each time I have successfully secured it, which shows either that I have a quiet native charm, or that they were pretty desperate for a chap.

One morning the clerk at Pentonville looked severely at me and produced a stiff card to take to an address in Clerkenwell, where (he told me) it would be exchanged for splendid employment. Well, of course, with my intricate knowledge of the London alleys (even those east of King's Cross, that curious no-man's-land, had not escaped me) I was able to take a short cut across the back of the New River Head and consequently arrived long after the head of the establishment had gone to lunch. So I went home to lunch myself, having prudently asked the way.

On my return I was ushered into a long shed which filled one side of a cobbled yard. I there found great activity going forward among a lot of girls cutting brown paper into a number of odd shapes and doing various mysterious things to it before finally packing the pieces into bundles of twenty. In the midst sat a gentleman in a neat suit and wearing a white beard. He gave me attentive audience while I explained my errand and at the end resolutely denied that he was in business as a Builders' Merchant. Then I was wasting my time and his!—but he thought not. Might not the employment he was prepared to offer be within my obvious powers?

Soon we were getting along very nicely; I told him I was a poet and he said he knew Dr. Joad. Before the end of an hour I was enrolled in the wholesale stationery trade. These bits of paper were being turned into newspaper wrappers with an

ingenious self-sealing device, and my job was to call on
stationers and "introduce" the line. I didn't have to sell it,
exactly—"It sells itself!"—but I had to get people to order a
few packets (or, if possible, a lot) and then it was hoped they
would automatically include the wrappers in their next order
for envelopes and H.B. pencils and the other things stationers
sell. Our wrapper was "distributed" by a famous firm of paper
makers and I was permitted to announce that I represented
this firm. Whole forests, I knew, were earmarked for the
manufacture of our fine "bonds" and "wire-woves" and
"cream-laids", and here and there a couple of trees would be
turned, at last, into self-sealing wrappers. The only thing my
new employer stipulated was that I should get a new overcoat,
which I suppose he thought would effectively conceal my other
rags.

Wages? Well, there were no wages, exactly. I worked on
commission, and if I could sell only two or three million
wrappers a week I should be in easy street. We had a long
discussion about this: easy street was not my immediate
objective, I explained. I needed food and lodging from day to
day (and a little over to buy books). So we agreed that I should
have—what was it? a pound a week, I think—enough by way
of advance on commission yet unearned to enable me to earn
it. And the overcoat, if I remember rightly, was also charged
against future successes.

Betty and I carefully chose this overcoat after trying on
pretty well every thirty-shilling garment in London. In the
end we got a bright blue one in Charing Cross Road, and for
good measure I bought also a pair of striped trousers, rather
like those natty ones city men wear, only the stripes on mine
were half an inch wide. These trousers were somewhat short,
but they were suitably cheap. By turning the turn-ups down
I made them do; but I had to be careful about holes in my socks.

Charles lent me a suitcase for my samples. In those days the
brief-case which is now every traveller's badge had hardly
come into fashion. Rich travellers had them—experienced men,

turning over maybe twenty pounds a week—but many self-respecting commercials (and certainly I respected myself almost to a fault) were content with the same sort of blue cardboard suitcase as I carried. Did I also have an umbrella? I think I did: I must ask Charles—for no doubt this, too, would have been borrowed.

My first beat lay all round London's perimeter. I visited Richmond and Twickenham and Stanmore and Barnet and Croydon and Greenwich, leaving little caches of the self-sealing wrappers to mark my progress. Kingston, too—I mustn't forget Kingston. I sold a gross there.

Then, valuable experience gained, and the girls working double-shifts having built up again the stocks my successes had depleted, I moved out into the Home Counties. The Green-Line routes began to know me, and the cities, towns, steadings, in that great network of public services, were soon familiar with the blue coat, the blue case, and the rolled umbrella, if I had one. Hoddesdon, Ware and Tring; Watford, Rickmansworth, Hertford, St. Albans. Reigate and Redhill. Rochester. If there was a castle, or cathedral, or both, to be inspected; if there was a museum, or an antiquity or two, or a fair, or a walk by the river; above all, if there was a bookshop, I counted the day not lost. Nor did I neglect business; by my efforts the people of Staines, Gravesend, Elstree and Epping were soon posting papers and magazines hither and yon without any messy paste, gum, glue, string or sticky labels; and hey presto, the happy recipient was in possession of his prize with a dexterous flip of the wrist. Meanwhile the man in the blue coat moved on.

My next tour embraced Dover, Folkestone, Hastings (and St. Leonards), Eastbourne, and Brighton. I believe I was a completely new experience to the buyers in these towns. At Bournemouth I was able to tell the local branch that the Eastbourne branch had taken X dozens of grosses; and at Eastbourne I had already praised the enterprise of the buyer at Bournemouth. It was probably the same chap, but no matter.

And then, flushed with success and with enough commission

earned to make me the fully-paid-up proprietor of my overcoat, I was sent off to Leeds, with the prospect of proceeding thence to Glasgow. We bag-men get around, you know. Making my headquarters at Leeds in a very odd sort of lodging house I went off on day trips to Halifax, Huddersfield, Bradford, Ilkley-Otley (I never discovered the difference), York and Dewsbury. What a venerable old pile Kirkstall Abbey is! How I loved York Minster! Doesn't Halifax smell of toffee! In Wakefield I saw a Wedgwood vase for fifty shillings like one I had bought for 6d., and I hastened in to tell the shopkeeper. This was the first time, I think, that I ever heard an expression subsequently popular: "I couldn't care less."

That landlady in Leeds! I wonder what she made of me? She certainly allowed herself to be put out not a whit by my presence. She gave me very little to eat, and never made my bed. Twenty-five shillings, and all found, wasn't it? One of the things she found was a loaf of bread and a lump of that orange-coloured cheese, which I had smuggled into my room to stay the pangs of hunger. No doubt at the final reckoning this went down as corkage.

What brought my travels in Yorkshire to an end was an overwhelming desire to see Betty. I returned to London on a midnight train and presented myself unexpectedly at Head Office on the Saturday morning. Everyone was furiously turning out wrappers in readiness for the expected rush from Glasgow, and my arrival was greeted with polite dismay. I had no money, I explained; but I didn't let on that I also wanted to see my girl.

When everything was finally cleared up I was left with a few shillings in my pocket, a fine overcoat, and a nodding acquaintance with the coast resorts from the North Foreland to Selsey Bill. By Monday I was all set to get back on the dole, where I belonged.

I must insist, though, on a distinct understanding about all this. I was not then idle by nature (that came later). I worked pretty hard, as a matter of fact. I used to scrub out my room most weeks, and I used to run a lot of errands for Charles, and I typed out the whole of Ridley's *Marxism and Anarchism* on Charles's typewriter, and I wrote all those short stories that Pavey spoke so kindly of, and I spent long hours at the B.M. studying books of great rarity and obscurity. You mustn't think of me as a neer-do-well, I did very well in some directions, I can tell you. One day Ridley pushed a note under my door at midnight to say my Agent (our Agent, in fact) had sold one of my stories to *Time and Tide*.

So the very first money I ever earned by my pen was two-and-a-half guineas (less ten per cent.) It was a very *short* short story.

One result of all this was that I decided now I was an established writer I ought to be in demand as a reviewer; and what better place in which to exercise my talent than the columns of *Time and Tide*? So one morning I set off to spy out the land. The office of *Time and Tide* is conveniently near the Museum. I called, asked for the Literary Editor, gave my name —and was asked to go up. As simple as that. So up I went, and was greeted with polite surprise by Miss Theodora Bosanquet. Was I Mr. Hopkins? Indeed I was! But I was not Mr. Gerard Hopkins . . . Well, no.

The accident of my arrival just when Gerard Hopkins was expected proved a lucky one for me; for Miss Bosanquet generously gave me some reviewing, and I have enjoyed the pleasantest of relationships with the paper ever since. What nice girls they have! For one of them, Helen McGivering, I wrote many years later a little wedding song which is the rarest of my works, and one of the shortest. Twelve copies were printed of this "Bridal Song for Helen"—a happier fate than befell a similar Bridal song written for a poet of my acquaintance, who proposed printing a number of such tributes in a small book. Before the small book could be produced, his wife had left him again, and all I ever saved from the wreck of his marriage was two lines which I used later in another poem.

Goodness me, I wasn't one to let opportunities slip. During the war I was at an Educational Course at Watford. After one of the lectures, pausing only to tell Lord Hinchingbroke in passing that I considered the pay of Lance Corporals a scandal, I intercepted Mr. Kingsley Martin who was dashing to catch a train in order to tell him, with appropriate quotations, that the *New Statesman* would be all the better for a few of my poems. Mr. Martin and I ran down Watford High Street side by side, he listening and looking at his watch, me making the best case I could for myself above the thumping of my army boots. But I got a poem in type and I have the proof to support my story. I don't think the poem ever got into the paper proper; but at least I got paid. I never came across Mr. Kingsley Martin lecturing any more, and I have never been able to make up my mind whether or not it is in order for me to say I have been a contributor to the *New Statesman*.

Another paper I couldn't get my works printed in was *G.K's Weekly*. They had every opportunity, for I called regularly with piles of poems, and once met H. Belloc on the door-step. I knew it was him, but he didn't know it was me and the moment passed; all the same, it was nearly as good as being patted on the head beside the Round Pond by Holman Hunt.

I was well placed at Charlie Lahr's to know all the papers, for no matter how obscure a print might be, it found its way to him. Indeed, if there ever was a journal with so small a circulation as two copies there is little doubt that Charles would be among the subscribers. One of these very small publications was *The Democrat*, edited by Beatrice Hastings. Here was another remarkable lady whom I am proud to have encountered. The great days of the old *New Age* were gone for ever, but Beatrice Hastings kept the same faith and the same principles alive with hard-hitting good humour, and had a wealth of reminiscence with which to entertain unfortunates like me who had been born a generation too late.

Another journal I failed to write for despite every effort was *Courier*. This handsome periodical had just commenced publication, and one of the head ones was Gerald Kersh. I used to shuffle down to Trafalgar Square looking my leanest and most starved, with a bunch of sonnets or a story about bosoms, and Kersh used to press half a crown into my hand. Another friend of mine who never gave anybody half a crown in his life used to tell me Kersh was only showing off; and this, then and now, I absolutely deny. You can show-off, if you want to, without laying out any money. The fact is, Gerald Kersh is the most generous of mortals, whether rich or poor. I was able, many years later, to put the opportunity of some work in Kersh's way, at a time when he happened to be temporarily a little less prosperous than usual. Kersh rang me up to ask if his friend So-and-so could have the job instead.

In the matter of half crowns Kersh would not take no for an answer; if I happened not to have a hand free (which was seldom) he would press the coin into my top pocket. If he was engaged when I called he would send out a note, like this, wrapped round the coin: "Hopkins: terribly rushed this morning. Can't come out. *Have a drink.* Kersh." Several such notes are preserved among my papers; but they seem to have got separated from their half-crowns.

Kersh also introduced me to his publisher; and if nothing came of the meeting, that was hardly his fault.

Occasionally I would take a job for a time, if only in order to qualify for the dole again. One such job was with a publisher who (so far as I could tell) usually employed no traveller. But he had just produced a very elaborate work of scholarship in the form of a reference book dealing with certain aspects of the English novel, and this huge tome (for so it was) I had to "subscribe." I got six and eightpence for every copy sold and I sold altogether a couple of dozen copies. Big money, that was, for I already had my overcoat and my new employer didn't seem to mind what I wore. Fancy actually being *encouraged* to visit bookshops in the course of one's duties!

Another of my jobs was going round getting people to fill in forms for the voters' lists. This is highly dangerous work in a borough like Holborn, where quite a few of the inhabitants are wanted by the police. I can tell you, I reckoned myself lucky to get out of some of those tenement buildings alive. "Who lives 'ere? Mind your own bleeding business," they used to say, and I used to reply that it was the law, not me; then they would slam the door, or close the window, or shout " 'Ere, Bert!" to some fellow with big fists and a scowl. On the form it said, "The Collector will give you all the advice you need"—or words to that effect. But you try telling an ancient crone that her nine children are illegitimate, when she thinks only seven are; or that a "person resident in the house" is only anyone who will be actually staying the night there on Tuesday, May 7th, when Bert aforesaid expects to be cracking a crib in Hampstead that evening.

All the same, this work had its compensations. How gratifying to tap the door and discover that—purely in the course of business—you have stumbled upon Winifred Holtby. I bagged several authors in this way and carefully refrained from letting on that I was "one of us". As a matter of fact, now I had had a couple of stories published and about three poems (and a review) I was much less anxious to proclaim my genius. It must by now be apparent to all, I thought.

I was once mightily impressed by a remark of Eric Warman's in this connection. We were meeting some high official in one of the film companies (at least, Eric was; I was merely present as an underling. All these big shots go about with underlings in attendance and I used sometimes to go along to give Eric the proper status). Well, this important chap shook Eric warmly by the hand, nodded very civilly to me, and said, "Eric Warman? I've heard the name before somewhere?" To which Eric magnificently answered, "You may have done. I've published a couple of novels."

I went home and practised that: "*I've* published a couple of novels." Or, better, perhaps: "I've *published* a couple of novels." I found there were nearly as many ways of saying this as of saying the third line of Gray's *Elegy*. But, unfortunately, the couple of novels remained Eric's and not mine. One of them was just as much banned as Hanley's *Boy*.

making easy money this way; indeed, one was said to be making £50 a week, free of income tax. But I was determined to be loved for myself, and furthermore it wouldn't have surprised me to be paid in counterfeit money. I had always been brought up to a proper suspicion of foreigners.

All the same, I think my blue overcoat would have looked well at the altar.

I had now settled down comfortably and had wholly given up any idea of re-entering the builders' merchants' world, although I occasionally passed Pryke and Palmers in Upper Thames street with a mildly nostalgic pang. Mac, I felt sure, would speak a word there if applied to; and, unless I am greatly mistaken, this venerable firm offered the added attraction of delivery vans powered by horses (they had motors, too, no doubt.) And they had the fine river Thames running along the end of their back yard. But I hardened my heart. No more pullies, pedestal pans or three-quarter-inch gas barrel for me!

My solitude was pretty well as crowded as Jack McLaren's. The busy day over and Charles gone at last home, pedalling away to Muswell Hill on a bicycle just not ancient enough to be a penny-farthing, my night-life would begin, usually with cups of tea. Sometimes I would go to the pictures (a gallery seat at the Stoll cost 6d.). Sometimes I would go to a meeting at which Ridley was to speak; many such meetings took place at the Conway Hall, and after one of them I wrote to Richard Church to inform him that what he had said had been dead right. This must have been awfully gratifying to Richard Church! But his response then, as always, was unfailingly patient and kind, though he was under the stern necessity of affirming that because I agreed with him on some point connected (I believe) with events in Spain there was no real hope of the house of Dent publishing my poems.

Sometimes with tuppence in my pocket I would sally forth to occupy the West End. With my hands deep in my pockets and the scowl of genius on my face I would trudge along, preferably in the gutter, and look uncommonly and unnecessarily

9

furtive whenever I met a policeman. My hair used to stick up in all directions and none of the girls in Glasshouse street ever spoke to me. Perhaps they took me for one of themselves. As I moved through Coventry street and Leicester Square I would assure myself that the tourists, the rich Americans, the various well-dressed, coffee-coloured people from odd corners of the antipodes, certainly took me for a native, and probably for an artist of some sort. I sometimes regretted that I couldn't grow a beard; but going unshaven ever so long had practically no visible effect on my face, which is one reason why razor blades don't figure prominently in my household accounts. A penny blade lasted me indefinitely and would have lasted longer than that if it had not succumbed to the enroachments of rust.

I had a mouse in my room. He used to come along the shelves and eat the crumbs and Betty and I would watch him. One evening when I returned home he was in such a hurry to get away that he fell into the water jug and had to be wrung out and set back on his feet. I specially remember that evening because it was the one in which I saw the ghost. This was a woman's face in the air at about the height of one standing, but having no body attached; the face (says my diary) was "clear but unreal". It vanished, just as I was preparing (says my diary) to make what the papers call "a certain suggestion".

But the ghost Betty saw in similar circumstances appeared to be a man.

I like to think my ghost was Jane or Ann Taylor; and why not? The practice of appearing face first has the authority of *Alice in Wonderland* and my friend E. H. Visiak once met the face of Milton in a corridor.

But my days at Red Lion Street were numbered, for the upper room could by no ingenuity be made a permanent home for two, and about this time, sitting on an upturned dustbin in the basement area of an empty house in Queens Gate Gardens I had myself proposed marriage. There was no prospect of £50 going with this proposal, but Betty accepted it all the same.

The immediate problem after this was accumulating money

to buy an engagement ring. As you will readily understand, any girl having the courage and resolution to accept my hand would be the sort of girl to whom an engagement ring would not seem essential; but I was determined to do the thing in some sort of style. Perhaps Betty paid. Anyhow, we selected something rather attractive in Notting Hill Gate and I let it be known among my friends that changes in my circumstances were projected if not imminent.

Those who had seen Betty greeted my news with a mixture of envy and approval; the rest accepted it and changed the subject. To most of them, getting married was routine stuff; some of them had already done it four times.

Marriage and other Attractive Moves

Before proceeding I had better explain how it happened that I was able to get married in natty brown shoes and a black overcoat that had a little silver chain to hang it up by at the back.

I came to London in April, 1938, and I got married in September, 1939. These eighteen months I have discussed in the foregoing half dozen chapters, but I have left quite a lot out. For example, I see I have left out completely the girls Ann, Amy, Muriel and Margaret; but no matter. I have also left out Juan Nazarian and Boyne Grainger, both of whom were in London in the autumn of 1938. It was to Bonnie on her departure that I gave Scabbo, my bronze figure with the alleged concealed diamond. We had explored large tracts of London and surrounding parts together, me guiding and she paying.

About the same time Juan Nazarian was giving two or three recitals in London before returning to the United States after a European tour. We heard him at the Wigmore Hall, and again at the Aeolian, on the second occasion in the presence also of Count Geoffrey Potocki de Montalk. The Count noticed the concert, I fancy, in the next issue of the *Right Review*.

Well, when it came to sailing for America Juan's suitcases would not hold all his souvenirs; so a pair of socks and a pullover were left in my custody, and after his final departure I found also a pair of shoes and the black overcoat. I often wondered if he had taken off the socks and forgotten to put his shoes back on; but I didn't care to go to the expense of a cable just for that.

So I wore the overcoat off and on for some years, and then we had it turned and it came in for my father. The bright blue one I still have: wonderful value, that was.

In those days one of my ports of call was Max Blore's book-shop in St. Christopher's Place, Wigmore Street. Max used to maintain a box of 100 Woodbines on her desk and this was at the disposal of all those customers favoured with the entry to the inner room. She also had a tray of tea or coffee almost con-stantly about to be drunk; and this, too, one might share. It was here that I first met Penryn Chave, that formidable bearded contributor to recondite journals.

Round the corner in Wigmore Street Max had her flat: two rooms and a landing completely filled with books, and a kitchen-and-bathroom nearly filled. Here reigned Ambrose, a cat of unblemished character and highly individual talents. In the front room, looking down, down, down into the far-below bustle of Wigmore Street we would sit and drink tea-with-mint or tea-with-lemon while Max told stories which from a lesser mortal might have been thought improbable.

We would drink bottle after bottle of Cyprus sherry at 2s. the bottle *and tuppence back on the empty*; and let me tell you that was a very fine sherry for the money.

Max herself was a figure notable in any company and positively startling in some. Her face—and indeed all her skin—was a brilliant white, and her very abundant hair was an astonishing red. This was not a red to be described in terms of other reds; but other reds might be given status and lustre by being described as like Max's hair. Among her adornments was a rope of amber about nine feet long, consisting of pieces as big as pigeons' eggs. None but a woman of Max's character could have sustained the weight of this bauble. She wore rings which most women would have been proud to employ as bangles. I don't mean—Heaven forbid!—that Max was large in herself. Not a bit of it. She was—and is—a woman of so spirited a personality that the accident of a normal-size body would not prevent her, if she thought fit, from wearing coconuts for ear-rings. If some folks did that it would seem eccentric; if Max did it, it would start a fashion.

Well, this magnificent creature got run over and was whisked away, loudly protesting, to the Middlesex Hospital. This was a day or two before the outbreak of war and Max, I believe, always considered that the one calamity led to the other.

At all events, a message reached me to the effect that I must now manage the shop and occupy the flat, for the proper maintenance of the business and the sufficient comfort of Ambrose. All these things I did and I stayed on even after Max, having practically taken the Middlesex Hospital to pieces with her bare hands, had been permitted to leave; for Max was delivered to the care of Mrs. H. Pearl Adam, who lived just across the way.

Excellent Persis! None could calculate to how many you have been a friend in need! The flat in Wigmore Street accommodated all who came, with beds, meals, the best of conversation, the company of Micky and Peter, those princes among cats, the solace of a wireless set so venerable that one expected it to announce the news of the Flood, and a hundred other amenities. Through it all, entirely unperturbed, moved Persis, getting on with her weekly page for the *Sunday Times*, writing other articles, and books, preparing meals, pouring drinks and giving forth delightful reminiscences of Kipling, Orpen, Raemakers, and many other fine chaps.

Here in the Green Room Max was now established, and held her court. To her daily were carried news of Ambrose and the first editions and when it became apparent that she would be out of action for some weeks I moved finally and more or less permanently into her flat, giving up the room in Red Lion Street, though not without a pang. A young woman moved in to succeed me and I lost for ever the right to mount to that upper room. I was no more now than one loiterer among many in the central four-foor-square of the shop. But even this for the moment was denied me, while I was busy looking after the bookshop in St. Christopher's.

Betty and I now prepared to get married. Max's flat was just the thing for us, we decided; and after all a bookshop manager is a very different marriage-proposition from a poet on the dole.

We had some difficulty getting witnesses for this ceremony. I telephoned several people without success—one was leaving town that morning, another had a cold in his head and yet a third could not be absent from his place of business on pay-day. In the end Penryn Chave and R. B. Marriott accepted the office and attended to discharge it. The other onlookers included two or three people who were waiting for the next wedding, and Betty's friend Sylvia. All this took place at the Town Hall, Marylebone and the man ran after me at the end to congratulate me and get a tip.

Persis had insisted on providing a wedding breakfast and with Chave in attendance we returned to Wigmore Street. Here awaited us roast grouse and other dainties, to which for good measure Persis added a bottle of champagne. This over and without even being allowed to wash up, we adjourned to Max's flat for our honeymoon.

Here is a list of wedding presents copied from my diary; it is not absolutely complete, but it gives a very good idea of what we had to set up house with. In some departments it was specially strong, but notably lacking in things of every-day utility.

Gifts so far:	7 wine glasses	Mrs. H.
	1 wine glass	Mrs. H.
	4 wine glasses	Mr. Chave
	2 decanters	Mrs. H.
	1 nightie and £1	Mrs. M.
	1 brass teapot	Mr. Chave
	1 brass tray	Mr. Chave
	1 wedding ring	Max
	5 silver knives	Max
	£1	Paul
	6 ashtrays	Mrs. Adams
	1 set lace mats	Max
	1 book (poems)	Charles
	1 tapestry match box	Mrs. Streen
	1 ashtray	Mr. Hoskings.
	1 glass pot	?
	1 set coffee things	Mr. Mushlin

1 set tea things	?
1 coffee pot	?
£1	Louis

While I am about it I may as well copy the final entry from my diary, dated November 29, 1939: "Touched Kersh for 2s. today." I am quite sure this is untrue, for Kersh never waited to be "touched"; he always had a fistful of money as soon as I hove in sight.

This list of gifts is interesting; it does not include gifts received from our families and from friends (Paul apart) at Bournemouth, or at Langold, where Betty's people lived. These came later and included at least two sheets, I know; because for a long time they were the only two sheets we had. Mrs. H., so prodigal with wine glasses, was the keeper of one of St. Christopher's many antique shops; so were Mrs. Streen and Mr. Hoskings. Mr. Mushlin was the bookseller, expert on Bernard Shaw. That nightie was entirely transparent, like a whisp of cigarette smoke curling round the wearer's body, very enchanting but not very warm.

Now while the newly-weds retire to enjoy their own society, coupled with that of Ambrose, I will describe St. Christopher's Place, for this was to be our home.

St. Christopher's Place is about forty yards long, and it runs from Wigmore Street—opposite the junction with Marylebone Lane—to the cul-de-sac of Barratt Street. Beyond this, changing its name and getting ever narrower, it ventures on another thirty yards to Oxford Street, coming out opposite Bond Street tube station.

Each side of St. Christopher's, which is all pavement and admits no traffic, are little shops. Most of these are antique shops, but in our day there were a boot-repairer, a vegetarian restaurant, and Max's bookshop to relieve the monotony of framed samplers, toby jugs and near-Chippendale chairs.

Above the shops was the warren of apartments known, very properly, as St. Christopher's Buildings. Those on the east side were older and rather smaller; those on the west shot up like a cliff and housed goodness knows how many old spinster ladies and a number of robust families too. The front shot up like a cliff, I have said; and so it did. But the back—reached only through a narrow arched passage—was rather like those terraced dwellings they have for certain animals at the zoo. A row of iron balconies ran along, one above the other, to the number of five, and these were reached by a staircase in a central tower detached from the building proper. You sometimes see such things in American films about Paris. Opening on to the balconies were the suites of chambers, one- or two-room, and presently in No. 48 we were enabled to set up our first separate home. No. 48 was a one-room apartment. It was about ten feet square, and because it happened to be opposite the staircase it was rather dark. The window looked out upon the entrances to the communal lavatories—four to a floor—which also were accommodated in the staircase tower; and on the communal tap which served ten or twelve households, when it was not frozen.

The amenities of 48 included a small gas cooker, a gas jet for lighting, and a built-in coal box which would hold a hundredweight and had to be filled once a week. The coal-men, we found, exhibited no lust to climb the stairs, especially as the coal cart itself had to be halted in Wigmore Street. Every hundredweight of coal had to be carried about a quarter of a mile, as it seemed towards the end of the journey, and most of the way almost vertically uphill.

Having had the luck to get this accommodation—it was four and sevenpence a week, unfurnished—we had to buy furniture. No doubt you think a room ten feet square can be furnished easily enough; but it must be remembered we had to do it on about three pounds.

Our first purchase was undoubtedly a bed; a four-foot spring on four legs, with a cheap mattress on top. This cost something incredibly small like twelve-and-six (free delivery within the London area; and payments spread over eighteen months, for all I know.) Then we got a tall cupboard with shelves for £1. A chair or two (I can't tell you much about them because later on when we were particularly hard up we burnt them to save buying coal). A combined cupboard washstand with a shut-down top you could put a vase of flowers on. Bucket, kettle, etc. For five shillings we bought about sixty pieces of a dinner service in Rupert Street. We had all sorts of refinements besides our rather ostentatious show of wine glasses: we had a clock, for example, which Max gave us; it had no glass, but it kept good time for years and went right through the war with me and emerged still ticking, and having lost only about three minutes. We had a three-cornered cushion, and an enamelled bin marked "BREAD" and many other possessions. Having hung a piece of sacking over our window and lowered the gas to save money, we could go to bed absolutely surrounded by luxury; or so it seemed.

To this haven I brought Betty at the end of our honeymoon. Before many weeks had passed we managed to secure a larger apartment on the fifth floor—No. 72, with two rooms. This was at the far end of the top balcony and once a week it commanded an astonishing view: everyone came out on to the various balconies with their mats and rugs and shook them over the edge, so that the basement area below was left ankle deep in match-ends, fag ends, bits of fluff and hairpins. An incredibly ancient crone who lived rent free in one of the catacombs (I believe) used to issue forth and pick this miscellaneous mass of portable rubbish over for salvage. She must have had far more hairpins than a woman almost completely bald could ever hope to use.

Goodness how happy we were! Night and morning I would fill the water bucket, and then we could be completely private for the day. No-one had occasion to pass our door, for we were at the very end, and the inner room had no door to pass, anyway. It looked out and down into the court, and across the roofs opposite towards Oxford Circus. Of course, getting coal up here was an expensive business; the coal itself was about one-and-seven-three a hundredweight; and carriage on it was another bob or so. But anyhow we didn't burn much, except in the terrible winter of 1940, when we used to lie in bed fully dressed with the gas on to keep the room from freezing. That time nobody had any coal because the horses couldn't come out to drag the carts. We burnt quite a lot of furniture that January and lived almost entirely on bread and soup. But I am going too fast—first we must get safely moved in.

This entailed something in the way of a house warming, to which were bidden various friends and to which came with these friends various of their friends. We sat down mostly on the floor and fine talk flowed till the early hours. Let me try to remember who came: I may not be quite accurate, but I think there were John and Anna Boylan, R. A. Worrall, F. A. Ridley, Andrew Stewart, Alexander Simmitch, and perhaps Mrs. Adam. It was quite in order to sit on the floor for we had just bought a new carpet for thirty-five shillings.

John and Anna Boylan were so enchanted with St. Christopher's that they at once made arrangements to take the next vacant place, and not long afterwards they became our neighbours. John at that time was writing serial stories for *Red Star Weekly* and other magazines of the same kind, and what he didn't know about handsome, keen-eyed men, suave foreigners, and fresh young English girlhood was of very little account. The pay was Twelve Pounds Ten for ten thousand words, and many's the time the arrival of such a sum has saved the lives not only of John and Anna but of Kenneth and Elizabeth; for we were rather like the old folks in Edmund Blunden's poem: "All things we had in common, being so poor." I remember one particularly welcome meal which we ate at the Oxford Street Corner House, complete with various wines and extras (did we not smoke cigars?) John manfully paying for everything. It was the first variation from bread and soup for weeks!

John was as indefatigable a collector of books as I, but with an important difference: he also read them. I never seemed to read the books I bought, though I suppose I did really. John had read practically every novel, biography, or critical essay

published in the past half century, and appeared to remember
every word of all of them. He also knew a lot of writers (in fact,
everyone we met seemed to know a lot of writers, but there
were always enough writers to go round.) The Boylans in their
two rooms and we in ours had between us more books, I
suppose, than all the rest of St. Christopher's put together. But
our neighbours made up for it with wireless sets.

The rent of No. 72 was seven and tuppence a week. But like
everything else, it went up. I don't suppose you could live
there today under ten bob. And I shudder to think what it
would cost to import a hundredweight of coal.

Discreet Retreat from *Cimex*

They were uncertain days. The war was a few weeks old and nothing much had happened yet. We left the future to look after itself and gave our full attention to the pleasures and problems of love. The little world of St. Christopher's continued placidly to revolve round the Pontefract Castle, on the corner, and the local high street—James Street—with its fishmonger, grocer, newsagent and ironmonger. You could live and die within fifty yards of Oxford Street and never see that important centre of civilisation; and quite a lot of people probably did.

When Max was sufficiently recovered to return to the shop she decided to move to the country, and she took a place at Evesham, down by the bridge. To this she, Ambrose, and some ten thousand books were presently transported, with me in attendance to knock in nails and lift heavy weights. Betty meanwhile was received into the never-failing hospitality of 104, Wigmore Street, and used to go to the pictures with Persis in a taxi.

When Max was pretty well established in her attractive little corner shop we learned that in winter that part of the town was frequently under about eight feet of water from the adjacent river, and all was to do again (if a phrase of Housman's may be pressed into service). Max accordingly removed herself to a point above high water mark and settled to ten or twelve years in the wilderness, keeping in close touch with London through the butcher who held the appointment of caterer to Ambrose. Rations for that eminent cat were despatched by passenger train at regular intervals. Max herself learned to live on the roots and herbs which (she reported) were the sole nourishment of the natives.

I think it must be confessed that Max cannot be understood literally in her statements about this ancient town; but on the other hand I have heard strange tales in other quarters. Was it not here that Rupert Croft-Cooke was under grave suspicion of being a German Spy because he owned an Alsatian dog?

With my occupation gone to Evesham I gave up the book trade and set up again as an author. I began to sell my short stories fairly regularly (i.e., twice a year) and even had occasional successes with poems. I now knew at least one writer who was less successful than I, and to him I occasionally offered a word of advice and encouragement on how to get into *The Star*, a newspaper from which I had recently received six guineas.

This may appear a pretty, but not an unprecedented sum. It was sufficient to keep us fed and housed for a month. Here is a specimen from Betty's household accounts, which she kept for several weeks in an old note book.

14/10/39			s.	d.
Sat.	Rent		4	7
	gas			6
	clock		4	6
	cheese and chips			4½
	beef		2	9½
	potatoes			7
	chest of drawers		3	0
	cheese, custard powder, cakes		1	0
	bread and stamp			6
Mon.	cinema and chips		1	2
	milk and bread			5½
	stamps and gas			8½
Tues.	dripping			3
	milk, bread, sauce			9
	bulbs			3
	chips			2
Wed.	apples and milk			4½
	stamp			1½
	bread			4½

Thurs.	milk, gas, razor blade		3½
	sprouts and parsnips		4½
	corn beef		4
	lifting bed etc.	1	0
	Woolworths	1	5
	chips and cakes		4

Some of these items must be justified. Four and six for a clock seems outrageous, especially as we already had one. But this was for repairs to my little alarm clock, a very good machine which I had for my twenty-first birthday and which, after nearly twenty years, is still keeping tick for tock with Greenwich and other important centres. I expect we needed the alarm so that I could get up earlier and write more stories. "Cinema and chips, 1s. 2d." meant we had to walk both ways to the Stoll, where two seats (without padding) could be had for a shilling. Please don't think we ate the chips in the cinema. They would be our supper, bought and eaten probably in New Cavendish Street on the way home. The chest of drawers is the one now in the top back bedroom, painted cream. In those days it was blue, and we bought it from the dustmen who used to set up a stall at the corner with whatever saleable items they had gleaned in their morning's work. As for, "milk, gas and razor blade, 3½d." at first sight it may seem that very little of these items could be commanded for so small a sum. But half-a-pint of milk cost 1½d., a blade cost 1d., and a pennyworth of gas would boil several kettles and heat a room ten feet square for quite a while.

Other surprising entries in Betty's accounts include, "sausages 5d.", "wine 2s." and "haircut 6d."

Our amusements had to be restricted to things that didn't cost much, the occasional extravagance of a visit to the Stoll apart. Every Sunday we would make for the Park to listen to the speakers, each of whom in turn had his chance to convert us to anarchism, communism, Roman Catholicism, or Bonar Thompsonism, that highly individual creed. After this we would walk by the Serpentine.

But our best entertainment was the inexhaustible show of London itself. Far and wide we went, especially where there were crowds as poor, as carefree and as happy as ourselves. To Petticoat Lane we went, and Hampstead Heath, and the old Caledonian Market, and the New Cut, and down to the Tower Bridge markets, and to Church Street, Edgware Road, then in its hey-day. In Soho we used to buy the most extraordinary things in bottles and jars, and when the occasion was uncommonly special we used to go into a Corner House and request the orchestra to play some favourite piece of Betty's. My own favourites could not be played by four men with a piano and three fiddles. My taste in music ran to the tremendous and could be satisfied only by the more noisy of Bach's fugues and a few comparable pieces by Rhineburger.

I wonder how we managed to turn our cheques into money, for I had no bank account in those days and the Church Street stall-holders would hardly be likely to take a cheque for a guinea in payment for twenty-four tangerines (threepence). What! you cry—setting the cheque matter aside—twenty-four tangerines for threepence?—nonsense!

You are quite right; now I come to think of it, it was twelve. On Saturday night, last thing, you could buy *as many flowers as you could carry* for sixpence, and a dozen tangerines for three-pence and all sorts of other fine bargains. The lights would be blazing at eleven o'clock and the street nearly as bright as day and the last lucky shoppers would be snapping up armchairs for three-and-six and bedroom suites for fifteen bob and the gentleman selling rock salt for soaking the feet would be practically giving it away in his efforts to benefit the maximum number of suffering mortals before midnight.

Alas, those days are gone. Most of the stall-holders are now so rich that they content themselves with opening for a few hours in the middle of the day and you can take it or leave it. As for reductions at the end of the day, with prices as high as they are now even a reduction barely brings some of the stuff within reach of the middle classes. Church Street has never really recovered from the bombing and the tide has flowed away to Portobello Road. I hope the live eels like the change of air.

I wonder how long we were at 72 before we discovered that the premises had other occupants? Several months, I think; as long, anyway, as it took them to eat their way through from next door. There is a Latin name for these creatures, *Cimex lectularius*, which the eleventh edition of the *Encyclopaedia Britannica*, I am sorry to note, calls a "disgusting insect." Its sole food, we are there told, is the blood of man; but Betty found our visitors were also partial to that of woman. The only cure, we were advised, was to burn everything we possessed and flee.

The household accounts for that sad week have vanished; but the heaviest item was undoubtedly for insecticide, in which we pickled most of our goods, so thoroughly indeed that for weeks everything smelled and tasted of parafin (or whatever the stuff is made of.) Another biggish item was for moving houses; it must have cost us all of ten bob to get the bed, the carpet, the washstand/cupboard, and all those wine glasses from Wigmore Street to Marylebone. But we did it. Such representatives of *Cimex* as survived were left clinging to the ceiling ready to fall upon the next tenants.

Our First Basement

To us habitual dwellers in London, W.1, it seemed now that we were living practically in the provinces. We were in N.W.1, behind Marylebone Station, in a snug basement in a quiet backwater, Blandford Square. The only sound at night was the rumble of the tube trains almost under the house, and we soon got used to this. At least they didn't bite.

One positive advantage was that from our house you could almost see the labour exchange; it was a mere two minutes walk away, in Broadley Street. It was while I was working for this branch that I wrote to the Minister of Labour and recommended him to take steps to improve the manners of his staff. In those days when there were many hundreds of thousands of unemployed it was customary to herd them like cattle and to treat them like slaves. All that is changed now, and almost the last outpost of studied incivility is the post office. I am told at "Employment Exchanges" (isn't that the new word?) you are now called Mr. and given a chair. I wonder if this has anything to do with my letter?

Blandford Square afforded every comfort. We had our own lavatory, water in the house, a bath upstairs worked by penny-in-the-slot, and a large room with a kitchen built under the steps that led up to the front door. Within easy distance lay the green lawns of Regent's Park and its sunlit waters (I quote from a story hitherto unpublished). And, of course, the exciting stalls of Church Street. With such a large room we were free now to start buying again and we could set off for the market with light hearts, knowing that if we bought a sideboard for seven shillings or a sofa for six, we had room to house it. But we kept the bottle of bug mixture ever at hand.

While we were at Blandford Square Betty got a job. Our

room did not provide employment enough for a young and active woman and her new work filled in the time. It would also be idle to deny that the money was useful. So off she went to Marble Arch every morning, and I stayed at home composing short stories. Betty was never home to lunch but now and again somewhere between twelve and three I would hear a gentle voice at the area railing, "Ken! Can I come in and fry a herring?"

This was John Symonds. For various reasons I was rather afraid of John. He was much cleverer than me, he had been to Spain, he had read real books like Freud and Kafka and Rilke and even Bukharin. He could read Russian, though not very well. Beside all this, a nodding acquaintance with the writings of John Pomfret seemed ludicrous. And if John had not yet had a poem in *Horizon*, he was just going to.

John had very prudently ceased to live at Tulse Hill, where an intimate understanding of Kafka counted for practically nothing, and had recently come to live in Hill Road, St. John's Wood, just across the way from Eric Warman. But he found the top flat in Hill Road rather lonely by mid-day, and I think he disliked the lingering smell of fried herring in his curtains. So on herring days he came to me. He would fry, and use my salt and pepper ("Have you got a bit of bread?") and then depart for a rendezvous with some girl leaving me to wash up and dispose of a singularly well-picked set of bones. But I welcomed his visits, for he was the only genius of my own age in those parts; and indeed when would John not be welcome to all the salt I have? In those days his masterpiece, *The Shaven Head*, was still nearly a quarter of a million words long. He worked at it, pruning, cutting, condensing, until ten years later he was left with an extraordinarily pregnant epigram. And so much for *The Shaven Head*.

The war was coming nearer to Marylebone. Sometimes it seemed nearer than it actually was, owing to the power of sound to travel through the ground. The only time we were thrown right out of bed was when Tussaud's Cinema was hit.

It was about four hundred yards away, but so far as the concussion was concerned, it might have been in the next room. Another nasty bump was when a load of live bombs went off outside the Great Central Hotel. Yet a third was when a furniture factory in Lisson Grove was the unwilling recipient of an oil bomb. I liked least the bombs that came down with a sound like a tin tray being shaken, but Betty reserved her chief disapprobation for those that whistled. We had our share of both sorts.

Well, most people know as much as they need to about bombs, and I will not go into the matter very fully here. But one thing none who saw it will ever forget was the packed platforms of the tube stations. We were just near the entrance to Marylebone tube and about 4.30 each day the old women began queueing with their blankets and bundles of household goods. As soon as dark began to fall they were admitted—the first sirens sounding—and they didn't re-emerge until fifteen hours later. And those platforms, with sleeping bundles of humanity ranged along the wall, and the trains going through, hour after hour, just beyond the sleepers' feet. Except on the night of the furniture factory fire we always protested that we preferred being knocked on the head in the comparative comfort of our own basement. But that one night we braved the tube, found it intolerable, and finally spent the small hours in the Coventry Street Corner House.

Meanwhile I had only two real contacts with military affairs— I am speaking of those early months of the war, and of the first few months of the bombing. One was Tank Adam, Max's friend and niece to Persis, who looked mighty efficient in A.T.S. uniform even *before* the war broke out; and the other was Penryn Chave, who joined the L.D.V. and remained an active supporter of the movement until Lord Croft made his unfortunate *gaffe* about pikes.

I was able to keep an ear to the ground and get *the real truth* about the war from Ridley and other friends in political circles. It was one of these who assured me (soon after Munich) that

Hitler's tanks were made of ply-wood and Germany only had seven barrels of oil (or it may have been seven million; but anyway it wasn't nearly enough). One morning I met Ridley at the Museum entrance. "This will soon be no place for poets," he remarked, "France has given in!"

Although I had no intention of getting mixed up in the fighting until they sent a posse to fetch me, I knew this time must surely come and I began to take thought for the future. Betty, I decided, would be better off in the country with her mother.

And meanwhile, all around us our world was breaking up. I believe I am the only one of our circle who served in the forces (and it cannot be claimed that I was a success) but the rest did what they could in their several ways, some by going to prison, some by accepting employment in various ministries, one or two by becoming the male equivalent to Land Girls, and the Count by proclaiming himself King of Poland and thus settling the problem. Incidentally, the Count greatly embarrassed me once, in the days when I was a lance-corporal, by parting from me just near the War Office with a superlatively correct and utterly untimely Fascist salute. The feeble movement of my arm in response was as much a call for air as a valedictory gesture. And I bolted like a rabbit into St. James's Park.

Of course, I wasn't the only warrior; now I think about it, there were lots. John Gawsworth, for example, served in the R.A.F. and got his poems published in India, while the best I could do in the Army was publish an anthology in Belgium. Then there was Rupert Croft-Cooke in Intelligence getting mistaken for a spy on the other side. Still, the whole crowd of us barely made a platoon.

But all that was some way off. My next activity was in the Post Office where for three successive years I joined up at Christmas as an extra sorter. Most of us writers did that, and the five weeks of it represented the only certain income we enjoyed in the whole year. The first year—1938—I was at Mount Pleasant, but in 1939 and 1940 I was at Wimpole

Street, which was handier. I don't say all the extra sorters were unsuccessful novelists: some of them were fairly successful. But most of them were. I can't answer for the postmen, for of course we sorters considered ourselves a cut above them. Fancy going about wearing an armlet! We were allowed to dress and behave like civilians.

Just before Christmas 1940 Betty departed to the north to join her mother. I was to follow as soon as we had got clear of ninety-four million letters and six hundred million cards (a record). Meanwhile we gave up the basement and squeezed all our goods into a little room at the top of the stairs and here I camped out for a couple of weeks. Nearly everyone in the house had gone by this time, some here and some there, and it chanced that one evening when the sirens had been sounding off and on for hours there came several rather startling bumps round about Blandford Square and I was keeping my head well below the bedclothes. Then I heard a tapping at the door and the voice of the girl from the front room saying, "Mr. Hopkins, can I come and sit with you?"

Now there was a difficulty here. Ever since I read somewhere that Christopher Marlowe never wore pyjamas I had made a practice of sleeping with no clothes on, when I remembered and if it wasn't too cold. On this night, as it happened, there I was in bed with no clothes on.

So I snuggled down a little further and called "Come in" without much conviction. What she thought of my welcoming gesture, which consisted merely of allowing the tip of my nose to appear momentarily, I don't know, but all the same she chatted away to keep her spirits up for about an hour and then to the sound of the All Clear she departed. One way and another it was a strange encounter.

In that same small room, cluttered up with furniture, I sat for my portrait. This was painted by Mariella Keene, who was then practising from an apartment in Sutherland Avenue which could be reached at night only by picking one's way in pitch darkness over various heaps of rubble in Church Street,

Edgware Road, Maida Vale and Randolph Avenue. The portrait shows a face of infinite sadness and wisdom springing from the open neck of a red shirt. To help things along and not to put too great a strain on any one colour I wore a white-spotted blue tie, a green knitted waistcoat which had belonged to John Symonds, and sat propped against a yellow wall. The first sketch for this portrait was made in charcoal on a piece of three-ply and so pleased the artist that only our inability to get any more three-ply prevailed upon her to paint over it. While this painting job was going forward I was developing in my own branch of art. John Symonds, by precept rather than by expostulation, had set me to writing poems in the contemporary manner. I had noticed, too, that poems these days were always dedicated not "to" but "for" someone, even if they were a mere four lines or so. So, with a careful dedication "For" Mariella Keene, I composed the following:

> there is a carcase rotting in my bed
> while i am learning russian, and i think
> ah jesus go away! ah jesus, go!
> i flog myself to sleep, learning my russian.

This achieved for me a certain local celebrity. It was quoted in the pub at the end of Mariella's road, and John was pleased to approve it. I went steadily forward, emboldened by my success, and before long I could do it with one hand tied behind my back:

> my tongue's roots rot
> for nothing sweet among them
> soaks down a stain they will not seize upon;
> what feelers in this soil grow out in vain!
>
> has the hand purpose
> intent the hard heart
> knowledge the puerile frenzy of
> this brain?
> have fingers more the shape than they foretell?

All in all, the sad expression in Mariella's picture of me was doubtless justified; but it must have been a slip of the brush that achieved the look of wisdom.

Dustman's Day

Before I could look out my pyjamas and dust the room in readiness for any eventuality it was time to move houses again. We had arranged with a lorry driver who lived in Langold to pick up our goods one day when he was returning empty from London, and in due course he turned up in Blandford Square piloting a lorry some forty feet long with about sixteen wheels and sufficient deck space to land a Swordfish on. Our bed, table, chest of drawers, etc., made an inconspicuous hump under the vast tarpaulin and I looked out from the cab every time we went over a bump to be sure it hadn't bounced off. In this way—after spending about half an hour backing and manoeuvring to get out of the Square—did I turn my back on London after two and a half crowded and happy years. Off we went by those same roads by which I had come in—Maida Vale, Shoot-up Hill, Cricklewood and Finchley Church End. Little did I guess, etc.

Betty's mother lived at Langold, near Worksop, a mining village on the road to Doncaster. I have never finally worked out how many brothers and sisters Betty has, but between them they appear to be responsible for a large part of the coal output of the midlands. They also tend to have largish families, so that I am uncle to about four hundred strapping nephews and nieces, who provide a steady stream of twenty-first birthdays, weddings, christenings, etc., to be noticed.

We began by living with Betty's mother, whose principal ambition seemed to be to make each meal bigger and better than the last. I had never lived in the north before—and Langold is within a mile of the Yorkshire border—and I used to be rather frightened when I saw the table set for tea. It

looked as if all the food in the house were here assembled—
meat, pickles, dripping, salad, two or three sorts of jam, cheese,
cakes of several kinds, eggs certainly, cold pie, and very likely
stewed fruit and custard. The tea itself was served in vessels
such as I had never seen since the days of Uncle George at
Wallisdown: pots that held anything up to a quart, and were
supposed to be filled and drained at least three times before it
could be said that one had "made a good tea". So far as my
memory serves, we ate six such meals each day. The rest of the
time was one's own.

Langold Pit and village are comparatively new; they were
built in the late 'twenties, I believe. The streets and squares are
not unattractive in their uniform red brick, but in many ways
it was like living in one of the newer suburbs of a large town:
trim little houses all very much alike, in tidy streets lined with
small trees some of which had not survived the experience of
transplanting. In addition there was a small red-brick church
and a large red-brick pub and a club into which I cannot tell
how many barrels of beer disappeared weekly.

Round about Langold lay very pleasant country and some
delightful old villages. Worksop was about five miles to the
south and provided among other attractions three cinemas, an
excellent public library, a railway station from which after
many vicissitudes one might at last reach London, a venerable
priory church, and the gateway to Sherwood Forest and the
Dukeries. Northward from Langold lay Doncaster, a town still
not wholly horrible despite man's every effort, for it retains one
or two buildings left over from the gracious days of Dr. Dove,
in Southey's *Doctor*.

We had stored our goods in somebody's back room, but
after a few weeks we got a place of our own on the main
Doncaster road, looking across towards open fields beyond the
road itself, and giving a clear view of all that went on, which
at times was plenty.

The Pit itself lay some little distance from the village. It was
the first I had seen close-up, and with its big wheels going

round, and the tall slag heaps, and the little buckets going along on an endless cable, and various bursts of steam coming out here and there, it made a most impressive sight, especially on dull days. I thought these must be the sort of engines required for making a descent into hell.

In front of all this were set flowering shrubs, flower beds, lawns, and a cricket field. The miners worked in shifts, and there was always a thin trickle of clean ones going in and of soiled ones coming out. I was frightened of them, especially the soiled ones. But they left me alone, and one or two of them who moved on the fringes of our circle were even led to believe that I was clever.

At the far side of the cricket field, and a little apart from the main colliery, stood a long row of buildings. These were much older than the colliery proper and were once probably part of a farm hereabouts. They had now been converted into a club house, potting sheds, and so forth. And here was my tri-weekly port of call.

As I advanced over the fields trying successfully not to feel like a miner (there was no doubt I didn't look like one) I could see over the door a little notice board: "Ministry of Labour". I have drawn the dole here and there up and down the country in my time, and glad of it too, but never before in a cricket pavilion.

I used to enjoy those walks through the fields. Signing on was no hardship here. I missed the hurly-burly of Pentonville Road, and the never-failing discourtesy of Broadley Street, but in the main the rural scene pleased me.

One morning the clerk beckoned me to one side and said, "Have you thought at all of taking a job?"

As he said this a person by the door drew near us, and for a moment I thought I was going to be arrested. But he was the representative of my future employers.

"It's healthy work," he said without heat.

"Plenty of overtime," urged the clerk, unaware that he had said the wrong thing.

"You can knock up as much as three-ten a week," the stranger promised.

Pensively, I capitulated. It wasn't the three-ten, but I allowed myself to hope that after a few weeks or months with the Rural District Council I might qualify for a pension.

When I returned home Betty was a little surprised to hear that I had taken a job, especially when I told her I was going to be a Dustman. Her mother put out even more food for tea than usual; she knew all about the needs of those who live by manual labour.

Very much too early for my convenience the next morning I set out. I was to meet the dust cart and her crew down at the next village. I was rather shy. I felt too well dressed.

Looking back, I find myself somewhat handicapped in describing this chapter in my career because I can't remember any of these chaps' names, except one they called Ack. And Perce, the driver. But they were as friendly and idiosyncratic a collection of citizens as you'd find anywhere. And I'll tell you a strange thing: you know here in the south we smoke a lot of Weights and Woodbines? Well, up there they go in for Robins and Park Drive. I've seen a Worksop dustman go white with rage when he couldn't get ten Robins, just as a Metropolitan might if he couldn't get Weights.

Well, the way they work in those parts is like this: two men go in with a little trolley and trundle out the dustbins to the pavement edge. The lorry driver gives them half a street start. Then he brings along his lorry and the rest of the crew and they tip the rubbish into the lorry. A final chap on his own trundles the empties back. This is a lonely job unless you know the customers pretty well, and also exposes you single-handed to the dogs. But on the other hand there isn't any heavy lifting.

Do you know what these colliery people do? They fill up their dustbins with the lumps of solid rock that come mixed with their free coal. Accordingly, quite a small dustbin with a few innocent tea-leaves and ashes on top may turn out to weigh three hundredweights when you come to lift it.

My first morning I was detailed to assist Ack and sent on ahead to learn to trundle out. I had the little trolley and Ack with matchless aplomb trundled the dustbins out by hand. By God what a genius that fellow had! Tilting a heavy dustbin on its edge, he would propel it by an easy movement of the flat of his hand and wrist on the top of the lid, rather like you used to be able to see porters do with milk churns. My trolley had two wheels and a sort of double hook which hitched under the dustbin handles, after which one canted the whole thing forward and lifted the dustbin up. The offside wheel squeaked execrably and quite spoiled my pleasure in an otherwise innocuous operation. It was a little more difficult with dustbins with one handle torn off, and wholly impossible with old galvanised baths. A lot of people, for fun, I suppose, had dustbins with no bottom in, which could be trundled out by a careless operator leaving a long trail of peelings, ashes, bits of rock and baked bean tins along the pavement.

Halfway through the morning we knocked off for a bit of snap. I had not the faintest idea what snap was, and I suppose you haven't. It turned out to be food. We sat on a wall, or on the pavement edge, eating snap and disparaging the foreman— not Percy, our immediate boss, but the chief one at head office.

Percy told me I would have to join the Union, and showed me what to do. If I had refused there wouldn't have been a dustbin emptied for thirty miles round. He also showed me how to fill in a Time Sheet.

I don't want to give the impression that we country dustmen are slow chaps. We're quite as good as they are in town although we are not issued with cowboy hats. We had the most modern equipment, too. Our lorry went up at the sides like a fish-and-chip oven—come to that, it had a slightly fishy smell to it, as well. At the end of the day, especially if it were raining, we used to ride home in it with the covers down, and doing this felt rather like being inside the drum of some fantastic lottery. Ack and the others would sit round chatting, and every now and then as we went over a bump, a shovel or a pepper-pot of that curious pink powder would come sculling across the iron floor. By the end of the day everyone had some little treasure or other—for people often throw things away that are not a bit worn out. I found six or eight dozen razor blades once, obviously the accumulation of a lifetime, and hardly used at all. Then there's the kitchen fender, which looks quite nice now it's polished. Every trade, I suppose, has its little perquisites.

I discovered I'd need one of those enamel cans with a cup-shaped lid, for making tea in. Tea, by the way, is never "made" in those parts. It's "mashed". And tea mashed in a bucket is a very different affair from tea made in a pot—though mind you I've never tried it with China tea.

At the end of my first day I could smoke Robins and discuss the foreman with anyone.

We had two lorries, and several branch establishments. At one of these, in a couple of tumbledown barns, an old, old man who was past even trundling the empty bins back was busy all day sorting bottles into different piles, and bashing tins flat. He had a rough-and-ready press which would squash tins and make them up into a sort of square cake, ready to be sent away and made into new tins again—or bombs, I suppose, in those days. He also pottered about putting cardboard boxes into heaps. When the rain dripped through the roof he used laboriously to shift all his carefully stacked cakes of flattened tin to make room for the cardboard before it got wet; and then the foreman would say, "Don't put that tin there, or it'll go rusty," and it all had to be shifted back. No one ever thought of mending the roof.

Another of our outposts was the Corporation tip, a wild barren spot inhabited by one old man who sojourned in an open-fronted hut not much bigger than a sentry box. The first part of every day he spent collecting sticks for his fire, and after that he was employed in keeping the tip tidy. That is, he went round after the lorries had tipped their load, rake in hand, looking for rats, and occasionally he levelled the ground a bit. This was a rugged old man like a latter-day Lear and I greatly admired him.

One day—it was the winter of 1941, when we had all that snow—we went off in a body early and didn't bother with dustbins. We had a shovel each, and we drove out to the tip where the snow was four feet deep and began digging. I worked like one possessed. I was convinced we were digging out the old man. But he turned up from some corner at snap-time, and I found we were only digging a road in for the lorries. The tip, of course, was always on fire underneath, and it was odd to see smoke curling up through the covering snow.

Now this is the way you lift a full dustbin up: two chaps stand one each side of the dustbin, which is beside the open lorry. With their backs to the lorry they each lift a handle of the dustbin, with a "Hup!", at the same time catching it underneath with the other hand, and tipping it over their shoulders into the lorry. It sounds complicated, and perhaps I haven't got it right. I didn't always get it right in practice and then Ack would lift me and the dustbin into the lorry, my "Hup!" coming just too late when I was in mid-air. All the same, I've lifted hundreds, I can tell you. You had to be careful the lorry didn't drive on while you did it, but Perce was very considerate.

In these rural districts, of course, it isn't only dustbins that have to be emptied, but the principle is the same. Occasionally when Ack had disappeared behind a little outhouse and discreetly lifted the small trap door you would hear a respectful, "Pardon, madam!" but it hardly ever happened.

You wouldn't think chaps would have to work overtime emptying dustbins, but we did. Some of our best men had already gone to the war and we were terribly understaffed. On the other hand, people seemed to be chucking out more and more cabbage stalks, ashes, and baked bean tins. At one time there was talk of working till midnight with flares, but it never came to anything because of the blackout. And daily I got more and more muscular and like one of themselves, they told me.

A few days before I received my calling-up papers for the

Army I got the sack. It was some system they had—the chaps told me—of getting out of having to re-engage me after the war. No doubt it was nothing of the kind. But anyhow I never actually qualified for a pension. What I did apparently qualify for was a share in the local comforts fund. Right through the war I received at regular intervals a tube of toothpaste, a block of chocolate, and twenty cigarettes. Quite often they arrived without being squashed to pulp, which to a chap like me, with my experience of the post office, always seemed a miracle.

I suppose when dustmen see me now they look upon me as just another civilian.

Pantomime Private

I think it was Bett Harrison who told us the date just in time to prevent me joining the Army a day too soon. It seems unlikely that anyone would do that, but I very nearly did. I had already eaten a double-sized breakfast, and got my parcel of en-route snap packed, and looked out my railway warrant. It never occurred to us that the twenty-first was tomorrow, and when Charlie came home from the pit that night and found me still there he thought I'd deserted.

So next morning the whole business had to be gone through again. I thought as the bus took me away from Langold at last and I looked back, that I had never seen anyone so alone and unprotected as Betty. It is always much worse to be the one that stays behind. There was nothing to be done, so I addressed myself to the business of getting from Worksop to Derby, which was accomplished by changing trains at Sheffield. It was only the first of many nightmare journeys undertaken during the next five years. Of course, no journey that includes both Derby and Sheffield can be considered pleasant.

Some people seem to know all about the army *before* they join. I was not one of these lucky souls, but I came upon my first example of their methods on arrival at Derby. About a dozen of us had gradually banded together on the train and agreed among ourselves that we were bidden to the Depot of the Sherwood Foresters. There appeared to be nobody to extend a welcome when we came out of the station at Derby, so two or three of the timid ones, me prominent among them, asked the way to the Barracks, got a trolley bus, and within twenty minutes were safely under lock and key. The others, with oaths and virile cries, had all disappeared into a pub.

They'd catch it, we told ourselves. But they didn't; they turned up about half past closing time that night, comfortably merry, and greatly disturbed me and the others by getting into the wrong bunks and generally raising hell. All the Corporal said was, "Now then!" and the Sergeant never even appeared.

I don't suppose anyone wants to hear about my six weeks' basic training. It became increasingly apparent to me as the days passed, and to my instructors, too, I think, that I would never be a soldier in any of the better senses of the word. I was not so bad as the chap who saluted with either hand, according to the way the object of his homage was pointing; nor so bad as the chap who always stepped off smartly with the wrong foot (I forget myself now which one it was). That chap was a real problem: they could do nothing with him, although he was touchingly eager to oblige. He practised marching long after the rest of us had gone on to weapon training, map reading and other advanced matters.

But I will at least make it clear that by the end of the six weeks I had caught up with those who "knew all about the Army". I could dodge with the best, knew when it was safe to say "Sarge" and "Corp", and had sampled almost every kind of leave except embarkation. There was no competition for that. 10535392 Hopkins, K., was me. 10535393 Hopkins, S., who slept in the next bed, was no relation. But he was the only kink I have ever had with the town of Melton Mowbray. We were great friends by the time our training was over; and then the changes and chances of this mortal life (which are even chancier in war time) parted us for ever.

And what did six weeks at Normanton Barracks do for me? They taught me the rudiments of the Bren gun (which, however, the sergeant thought it prudent not to let me fire) and they gave me an opportunity I might otherwise have missed of forming the beginnings of a dislike for Derby which the next couple of years confirmed. Yes, two years! For when the six weeks' training was over and those who survived it were gloomily predicting that our next port of call would be

11

Alexandria or Wake Island, half of us were posted to Chilwell and the other half to Derby, where the R.A.O.C. had depots. I remained in Derby, at what was then called (I never knew why) No. 2 M.T.T.S.S., R.A.O.C. We all marched out of Normanton Barracks behind the Sherwood Foresters band and kidded ourselves we were soldiers.

Sunnyhill Camp lay on the southern outskirts of Derby on one side of the railway, and the Ordnance Depot lay on the other side, just across the way. Here was maintained a vast store of motor parts—practically ironmongery—but I never let on that I knew anything about such matters. I was rated as a storeman, third class, and I didn't reckon one and six a day entitled them to pick my brains. To give them their due, they never attempted to do so. Indeed, they hardly seemed to know I was there. "Pick 'em up!" they used to say, meaning our feet, but even that was addressed to everyone. I went for about three weeks without being individually addressed by anyone above the rank of corporal. If I'd known then what I know now I'd have kept it that way.

Then all of a sudden I was whisked away from the tyre section where I had been trundling tyres about like hoops and occasionally receiving a nod either approving or admonishing from higher up. Whisked away to be a clerk in the P.R.I.

The P.R.I. looks after various aspects of welfare and controls funds which "belong" to the men. From these funds are purchased various alleged comforts like football jerseys, a motor lawn mower, apples and so on. The clerks in the P.R.I. do the best they can for themselves in conditions not decisively unfavourable.

I was now removed from "F" Company and installed in "A" Company, the Headquarters Company. I found myself among the cooks, orderlies, policemen, batmen and other privileged mortals. As soon as they discovered that I could do things for them, they began to do things for me. I could get in or out of the camp at any hour of the day or night, and no questions asked. I had friends in the telephone room, where they had a private system for making tea. I had access to the cookhouse, in the remoter parts of which things were prepared and eaten that the outside world knew nothing about. I even had allies in the sergeants' mess, able and willing to supply bottles of gin, if not of whisky.

Off we used to go in the P.R.I. truck, to collect barrels of beer at Burton, or to buy mistletoe and paper chains, or to deliver some little dainty at the house of an officer. For the best part of a year I was a very willing assistant in this manifestation of the local war effort.

I sent off to Langold for Betty, although my presence was about the only attraction Derby could offer her. We were never in a less hospitable, or more ugly town. The only refinement of beastliness the authorities could think of they speedily added: this was the smoke screen, which while it blotted out miles of mean streets, and was thus a good thing, also filled one's stomach and lungs with intolerable fumes, which was a bad. Fortunately, Sunnyhill was not considered worth saving, and therefore had no such protection.

At first we lived in a furnished room with Mrs. T., who—with Mr. T.—afforded a model for my undoubted powers of mimicry. They were a very odd couple who used to sit motionless for hours one each side of the fire and very occasionally say, "Mmm", in a peevish mumble. I suppose that's what happens if you live in Derby long enough.

When they couldn't stand us any longer—let's put it that way—we went to live in another furnished apartment. The family here was much more friendly (indeed, almost the only friendly souls we encountered in those parts—at least among the natives). Betty thought it a little odd one morning to come down and find Mr. —— doing Swedish exercises in the kitchen with no clothes on; I was both surprised and pleased on going to have a bath to find the bath already occupied very prettily by the youngest daughter; but after all a fanatical use of locks and bolts can be carried too far (as I told Betty) or not far enough (as she told me).

Finally we got a pair of unfurnished rooms and settled down to a more or less normal life, the same as a couple of hundred other lucky people at Sunnyhill. Most of the H.Q. staff had sleeping-out passes and the accommodation thus made available at the Camp enabled the same number of extra slaves to be accommodated. "Slaves?"—well, so they thought themselves as they marched to and fro from the camp to the depot. Once a week they went a long way round, with the band playing; but this treat came out of their own time: work began at the usual hour.

I used to go to and fro on the P.R.I. bike, and I soon got in the way of turning up at the office about five to ten (just before the officers began to trickle in) and of leaving about five (just after they had finished trickling out).

The P.R.I. expanded with the unit; soon we had a couple of thousand men, and our department handled more and more apples, football jerseys, free beer and paper chains. My own share in all this was increasingly on the entertainments side. I teamed up with John Huxley and Ronnie Laws in writing and producing pantomimes, revues, plays, concerts and socials.

My colleagues were professionals, John on the legitimate stage and Ronnie in music hall. My job was to provide a bit of tone (they told me) to the patter and dialogue they prolifically devised. We made a good team, and put on some mighty fine shows, marred every time only by my inexplicable inability to persuade them to include a pet line I had written, and thought exceptionally apposite: "Number off for England!" But they wouldn't have it.

We all took part in these shows, wives as well. Betty was working at the depot by this time. (And so were most of the other wives. It was indeed almost a family business.) In one revue, Betty, dressed up like a hambone, had to stand and look decorative (which she very well knew how to do, and needed no training) while Jim Metcalfe sang a sentimental song. This went off very successfully. Another time she was decked out like Lady Jane Grey in what the Colonel unaccountably called the "fine ale" while the united company sang either Land of Hope and Glory or some words of mine to a similar tune, I forget which.

I myself was never allowed to star, but I made a great hit with my line "Alms for the love of Allah!" and always I was cast for screams and groans, off, even if a scream had sometimes to be written in specially to keep me happy.

One or two of the more successful pantomimes and revues we took on tour in the neighbourhood and we even staged them in the town for the entertainment of the civilian population.

These things did not occupy all my time, and I decided to go into publishing. After all, letters was my main business, not the theatre. I was encouraged by James Guthrie, one who had spent most of his life preaching that the artist should be less at the mercy of the middle-man. J.G. could write a poem, illustrate it, set it up and print it, bind it, and indeed do everything from start to finish. He recommended me to do the same, but of course I hadn't his range of talents. More modestly, I mean more unambitiously, I found a local printer and launched The Grasshopper Broadsheets as a means of printing and circulating my poems, and those of a few friends. At first these monthly broadsheets circulated mainly among my own circle, but after a time we began to sell them extensively, and at one stage had about two hundred subscribers. Between 1942 and 1945 fifty numbers were issued, and offered poems by established poets as well as by comparative beginners. Our stars included Charles Williams, Seumas O'Sullivan, Sylvia Lynd, Sylvia Townsend Warner, Stevie Smith and R. C. Trevelyan. When all else failed, and I was ashamed of too frequent appearance of my own name, I wrote under various other names. Still people supported us.

These sheets were folded and posted off each month; which means that a set in fine condition, and unfolded, is a bibliographical rarity. How lucky that I am still in a position to supply the first two or three hundred enquirers who approach me, cash in hand.

These broadsheets brought me a number of new friends—
Arnold Vincent Brown, Nancy Cunard, E. H. Visiak, Clifford
Bax, Brian Hill, Alec Smith, V. S. Wainewright, John
Butler—no, not John Butler: he was me—and Charles Williams.
And James Agate.

James Agate wrote a review of the broadsheets in the *Daily
Express* quoting a poem by James Guthrie (who was somewhat
his senior) and going on to say what such young men should do.
But it was all good fun, and the controversy was continued (as
most of Agate's controversies were) in the next volume of *Ego*.
Although, quite reasonably, he gave himself the last word in
Ego (but my last letter, the unpublished one, really demolished
him!) I took a splendid revenge by reviewing the book in
Time and Tide. He said it was the best review he ever had. I was
rather pleased with it, too: in about four hundred words it
embraced seventeen quotations or allusions—none of them in
French. In order to demonstrate to myself (nobody else cared)
that I could do this sort of thing just like Mr. Agate I pressed
into service Chaucer, William Morris, Myself, Belloc, Drayton,
Shakespeare, Praed, Humbert Wolfe, Johnson, S. Butler the
elder, Theodore Hook, and Cowper.

Of course, the war went on as well. One day I found myself
back at Normanton Barracks, which the Foresters had obligingly
handed over to us, since their chaps were now all busy fighting.
What a triumph, to be walking those remembered halls in a
pair of light shoes, and no anklets web; talking as man to man
with the Adjutant; nodding with easy patronage to junior
N.C.O's, and calling senior ones "Bob" or "Jim". I counted
myself one of the most influential privates in the battalion,
though perhaps not one of the richest. That distinction went to
a colleague down in a little shed, well off the beaten
track, who was selling bicycles as fast as he could build them.
Another chap who was doing well had a draper's shop in Civvy
Street and supplied huge quantities of tea-cloths, etc. They had
enough of those in the Officers' and Sergeants' messes to paper
the walls.

Other chaps who were on a good thing were those with talents in the sporting way; we had a heavy-weight boxing champion, several professional cricketers and footballers, a channel swimmer, an international ping-pongist, and of course dozens of actors, singers, concert pianists and the like. Luckily, I was the sole representative of literature and so long as my talk, though big, was vague, I was safe enough. And I did once get a letter with a literary agent's name on the envelope. No footballer was ever in any danger of posting in the winter season, and no cricketer in the summer; as for our water polo expert, he was careful to arrange fixtures all the year round and I suppose is there to this day.

Getting posted was, of course, what everyone avoided if possible, not because we loved Derby but because change in the army is usually for the worse. But for one reason or another, most of us were moved in the end, and (so far as I could learn by confidential reports) the pantomimes went to the dogs. For I—even I—was finally posted.

Was it the new Adjutant? Did the Colonel see in certain lines of dialogue allusions nobody intended him to take so much to heart? Or was it merely that bastard B . . .?

Almost before I had time to wipe off the grease paint, settle up my complicated affairs, bring back the P.R.I. bike, and predict ultimate confusion for that bastard B . . . I was in the train and on my way to join a Mobile Laundry.

Non-Combatant Lance-Corporal

I don't know who first applied the cant expression "Get mobile" to laundries, but about mid-1943 these units were springing up all over the place, as it seemed. My chief consolation as I sat in the train reviewing my present situation was that things would have to be considerably worse before laundries could be employed as a weapon. As a matter of fact (I learned later) the mere sight of one on the move could strike terror; and when it was working, with steam pouring from every joint, it was like a corner of hell. How they cheered as we first went through Rouen! It was our mysterious advent which finally convinced them the tide had turned.

I suppose I must apologise for being a non-combatant soldier. My martial spirit was perfectly in order, but I suffered (said the Sergeant) from trigger-snatch. This meant (and especially with a Bren) that I was liable to slay our side too. All in all, I was safer as a clerk (regimental) class three. Mobile Laundries maintained two such, a Sergeant, and (in this case, me) a second, with the appointment of Lance-Corporal. Ha!

From Derby to Wellington, Salop, in choice conditions is not a long journey. I did it often enough afterwards. But the first time it was a nightmare, because the Movements Clerk at Sunnyhill was an ex-L.M.S. man and he never used anybody else's railway if he could help it. So instead of sending me along to Birmingham New Street and permitting me to slip across to Snow Hill and get a direct train to Wellington—the whole thing would have taken about two hours—he produced a complicated route, mainly in local trains, by way of Birmingham, Stafford, and other remote corners, culminating ominously at a place called Trench Crossing. The only merit of this route was that it loftily ignored the existence of the Great Western.

And so I arrived cold, wet (no doubt) tired and hungry at Donington, there to be re-united with the stamp-collecting manager of Burgess's who was a Sergeant, of course. Everybody I ever met in the army whom I had known before the war was either a Sergeant or a Lieut.-Colonel. Some successively were both. The best I could ever do was acting-corporal. Oh, well!

Sgt. Harling was his name. He was some sort of important chap at the Mob Centre, but he passed out of my life again within about two days because we were shifted, us Mobile chaps, to Apsley Castle.

There was nothing much to do. Our Mobile Laundry was entirely new, beginning from scratch, and me and one or two more were the first arrivals. All we had to sustain our civic pride was a couple of tents and a name; no officers, even. But the food was good. Gradually more and more chaps were shown in to our couple of tents and at last an officer came up and looked at us wearily and went away. He looked tired, and had, perhaps, been sent to us by some outlandish method that utilised only the London and North Eastern; I don't know. Anyway, next day he told us he was in command, but he still had precious little to exercise his orders on. About a hundred men, and a corner of a field behind a cardboard ticket which said 215 M.L. & B.U., R.A.O.C. Those symbols! As soon as I got used to one set, they changed them.

Apsley Castle stood just outside Wellington and gave us a fine prospect of the Wrekin from our tent door. The countryside was charming, and the time of year summer—a dry summer, at that. Johnny Green and I used to go off for long walks along the banks of a canal, or to Much Wenlock, Buildwas, Iron-bridge—anywhere. Newport was another attractive place to go for tea. Then there were the various canteens and pubs in Wellington, which is a nice little town. And of course, the

Wrekin itself, that stupendous mountain. Sergeant Wright and I would walk that way, talking about women.

At last word reached us that our machinery was ready: seventeen lorries, four large trailers and six gennys, I think it was. Off went the drivers and the rest of us looked at one another with a wild surmise. Wouldn't be long now. Libya?

No, Witney.

When a new unit is being formed, various established units get orders to post men to it: six storemen, three sergeants, a corporal cook, and so forth With a cheerful cry of acquiescence the established unit sends off sixteen or twenty or fifty men as called for, taking care that they are the worst it has available; the jail birds, the cripples, the incompetent. How I came to be among them I have no idea. Anyhow, the next job is to weed them all out and get new ones.

To this we addressed ourselves. We had about a hundred and twenty men and we used to get them all lined up in the field and the O.C. would give a pep talk, or whatever everyone was assembled for, and then before moving off the Sergeant-Major would say, "Fall out, the non-marchers," and after a bit of a scuffle it would be seen that six hale fellows were left somewhat self-consciously standing under the broiling sun. A mob, indeed a rout of unfortunates, would be hobbling away in carpet slippers and leaning for support on the less decrepit of their neighbours. One man had two sticks and a whole sheaf of medical certificates to give them authority and another man had a curious malady which overcame him on parades and made him go practically on all fours, but happily left him in the evenings when he took his girl to the pictures.

At Witney I first learned to sleep on the office table, in order to be "near the telephone". You wouldn't expect Generals and the like to ring up a Mobile Laundry at three in the morning, but there was always a danger of it, so we had a Duty Clerk. As Harry Noble and I were the only clerks—for you couldn't count the sergeant in this connection—we took it in turn; but in practice we found it best to sleep permanently in the office, and this we did more or less until the end of our time in England. Overseas, of course, it was all different, especially after our telephone was struck by lightning.

I liked Witney. Far and wide we ranged, enjoying the view. Betty sometimes came down for the week-end, and other times I would make my way to Derby. I also, while at Witney, went on various "courses", taking care to pick the ones happening in or near London. Dear me, they were foolish enough to run one such establishment within a couple of hundred yards of Marble Arch; the lectures were very sparsely attended.

We had just got nicely settled at Witney, local liaisons progressing favourably, pin-up girls neatly arranged, pub closing times circumvented, when the order came to move. This time it was Northampton.

What a majestic sight is a Mobile Laundry on the march! It is hard not to break into a cheer as the mile-long procession goes by, Sgt. Wignall in front on his motor bike, then Lieut. Bradley in the 15 cwt. anxiously fingering a map, then the tall lorries and trailers, and at the end the O.C. anxiously muttering that he hoped Brad wouldn't miss the way. Naturally, the O.C. couldn't himself lead, for if the way were missed there had to be someone else he could blame.

Happily we were seriously inconvenienced only twice. The first time we went down a lane in Nottinghamshire which got narrower and narrower until at last it reached a hump-backed bridge about three feet wide. The cavalcade came to a halt while the M.T. Corporal measured the trailers and confirmed (perhaps in writing, with copy to Formation) that they were within an inch or so two-and-a-half times as wide as the bridge. Then, to the astonishment of several cows, some two hours were spent in backing and turning in a nearby field. Imagine the despair of Sgt. Wignall after we were finally re-established on the main road, to discover that the lorry that should have been running number five in the procession was now unaccountably at number eleven.

The other time was in Normandy, when we were to report

to some very high General for instructions. It had been expected that the O.C. would go alone for orders, but with guns banging and so forth he preferred not to be separated from his command, so he took us all along. We met the General when we were proceeding up the private drive leading to his chateau. There was no question of turning here. Inexorably we drove him back the way he had come, and as his staff car jolted slowly in reverse for perhaps a quarter of a mile, the General was neatly placed facing our way to outstare the O.C. There are times when a W/Lt. (Acting Captain) can blush as rosily as any private.

Northampton is a pleasant town and we were soon very comfortable there. You have to get comfortable at once in the army, or not at all. Before L/Cpl. Green and I had got to know the country really well for twenty miles round, but not before three of the lads had got engaged to local girls (or at least offered impressive future pledges in exchange for present favours) we received word to move. This time our destination was Farnsfield, near Southwell.

Farnsfield is a small village and I fancy our advent just about doubled its population—this remark has no hidden meaning. We were very happy there. The people liked us, and we liked them. I was especially well placed, for Derby was not hard to get to, and at Blidworth, a mile or two from the camp, Betty had a sister who was an unfailing source of food and hospitality. One day all day and far into the night droves of planes crossed over, making south. The war had suddenly come several steps nearer to us, and almost at once we took several steps nearer to it. Off we went again, this time to Upminster. Upminster is within easy distance of Tilbury; and Tilbury links up with most of the rest of the world. But at that time the majority of ships from Tilbury were bound for the same place: the coast of Normandy. Sgt. B. went about saying to everyone, "You'll soon be in the thick of it, cock," until someone reminded him that he, too, would be there. It was then that he was noticed always carrying (or even wearing) his tin helmet.

The habit spread, especially after the night the first flying bombs came our way. The very first was thought to be on our side and received something in the way of a cheer, subsequently covered up with a sort of nervous cough.

One merit which Upminster had (and still has, I rejoice to say) was its proximity to London. It is also, although the fact made a considerably smaller impact on our fellows, a good centre for those wishing to visit the tomb of Boswell's friend, and Johnson's, General Oglethorpe. I cannot say what the shade of that gallant officer would have made of a Mobile Laundry.

I spent much time in London during those few weeks, and I found flourishing there an association of poets and poetry lovers called the Saturdays, of which I was hailed as the Founder—to my surprise. To have Founded a society which, ten years and more after, is still much alive calls for some apology (using that word in the eighteenth-century sense).

One week-end in the previous March (it was now invasion-tide, June) I had telephoned Mrs. H. Pearl Adam, as my custom was when in London, to suggest a meeting. "Come to supper," said she. I explained that I was meeting a poet that evening. "Bring him," she said, "and I will provide another."

Accordingly along to Wigmore Street went Arnold Vincent Bowen and me, and there we found Vivian Locke Ellis and Persis. Now Persis will never admit to being a poet; but by an unaccountable accident, she has written a considerable body of work which the rest of us are content to call poetry. So we were four poets, or three poets and one, according to your point of view. For Arnold and I never swerved from the opinion that we were poets; and you had only to look at V . . .

That first meeting led to a second, and a third . . . and various people in one way and another got added to the roll . . . and so we have the Saturdays, which despite occasional schisms on the question of the pure Petrachan has gone from strength to strength

The credit belongs primarily to Persis, whose generous

hospitality in opening her house every Saturday to a noisy company anything up to thirty strong and all capable of reading their verses aloud far into the night has given a secure local habitation to the society. There is more than that to be said, when the society's history comes to be written. The next credit must go to Arnold Vincent Bowen.

Arnold was the only complete poet—in the sense I shall define—that I have ever known. Perhaps I may add that I have known at least a hundred poets.

Arnold lived for poetry; he read and wrote poetry for about sixteen hours a day and the rest of the time he dreamed about it. He was the full-time enthusiast. He would recite by the hour if allowed to do so. He would take infinite trouble over his own poems, or anyone else's, praising (always), criticising, revising, amending, restoring cancelled lines, cancelling others, polishing, exclaiming. Whatever the occasion he could see poetry in it. His *Lyrics of Love and Death*, the only collection he published before his sudden and tragic death in 1947, is still in print and ought not to be missed by the reader who enjoys "pure poetry" unconnected with fashion, faction, or the cliques.

One Saturday institution was the writing of a poem on a set subject in fifteen minutes. The title was drawn from a stock of such things and at the word go everyone scribbled away in frenzied silence for the allotted quarter of an hour. In that small time Arnold when in the mood could knock off anything up to a hundred lines, and close on his heels would come Arthur Ball. Other verse-making machines good for a fifteen minute epic were Robert Armstrong and Norman Pallant. I myself was never an enthusiast for Grey Books, as these writings were called. I like to await the visitation of the Muse in the solitude of my closet—as two unpublished lines which are waiting to have twelve others put in front express it:

> A lonely not a disillusioned heart,
> Fit harbour for the Muse, who dwells apart.

That was me; but of course ever since I wrote the lines disillusion-ment had been making steady inroads.

However, the number of these impromptus which have been published in respectable journals proves that the method that does not suit all is none the less sufficiently profitable to some.

Just as the Saturdays were really getting into their stride I found myself obliged to become a corresponding member. Sgt. B., almost completely encased now in armour of various sorts, began to issue sea-sickness pills. There seemed to be some prospect that the invasion of Normandy had progressed as far as it could without the aid of Mobile Laundries, and it was now our turn to be thrown into the contest. Thereafter there was never any real doubt of ultimate victory.

All the same, those pills were much appreciated.

Editing *The Bubblers' Journal*

There are few situations in which one can better study human nature than in the army. People are curious, as James Hanley noted in one of his book titles. And none more so than the personnel of a Mobile Laundry and Bath Unit. (This is the first time I have mentioned baths, I think. Baths are much in demand after battles. Our first customers included Ivor Novello and Diana Wynyard, who were playing in *Love from a Stranger* at Bayeux.)

Well, off we sailed one day from Tilbury and I took occasion to write a war-poem:

> Sitting on a paravane
> * With a bollard at my knee
> In a troopship off Southend
> Is not where I wish to be;
>
> But because these things are so,
> And there is no help for it,
> In a troopship off Southend
> On a paravane I sit.

This caused much difficulty to the O.C. when he came to censor the mail. Suppose the enemy had never heard of paravanes? Was it safe to mention Southend? Did the verses reflect a depraved morale? I fancy the complete poem never got through until after VE day.

We were three days in that ship: it was a "Liberty ship". The voyage passed without incident or excitement, except that one of the men was caught using a lavatory reserved for officers. By God it was lucky for him that flogging has been abolished. It was about a week before he could pluck up the spirit to go to a lavatory again anywhere.

As we pulled up a quarter of a mile or so from the shores of Normandy my career almost terminated for good and all. Everybody had to descend the ship's side by rope ladder and alight in a landing craft alongside. Fine. But to do this successfully with about two hundredweight of equipment hanging off one's person it was imperative that one should realize that this particular rope ladder had a rung which wasn't there. No such intelligence reached me before I found it out for myself the hard way. And the steel deck of a landing craft is uncompromisingly hard.

A little later we had a good laugh in which I was able to join. The drivers had all been on special courses to enable them to drive their lorries off a three feet drop into the sea and so to land. And the lorries themselves had been sheathed in waterproof material to enable them thus to paddle ashore. But when the great moment came the tide was out; down came the ramps, and off sedately moved the lorries, dry-shod and majestic. Nobody even bothered to drop a bomb in our direction. "Just you wait!" said Sgt. B.

We drove up through a shattered village to a marshalling area where I found time to shave in a puddle, feeling no end of a campaigner. One or two Candians shot at us, the usual very pardonable reaction to first sight of a Mobile Laundry. We settled down in the lorries or under them (but Sgt. B. is said to have rapidly dug himself a hole five feet deep) and snatched our first real sleep for nearly nine hours. And then Lieut. Y. discovered that the hammock he had stolen from the troopship was missing. So he called a parade of the whole unit and demanded the return of his property before he (or the rest of us) could sleep. But it was never found. At least no finger of suspicion could be pointed at me. Throughout that part of the campaign I slept in great comfort on the unit stretcher. I let it be known that it would pay any casualties to be walking cases; but as a matter of fact as soon as we were out of range of those Canadians we were never again in any real danger.

From that bit of high ground we had a magnificent prospect when morning came. The bay was one vast panorama of ships. Sgt. B. gloomily pointed out that several of them were upside down. Very much the right way up was the battleship *Rodney* which had the amiable habit of firing broadsides over our heads with a noise like the end of the world. A few days later we moved into the area where those broadsides had been falling. With that scene before us we earnestly hoped *Rodney* had been informed that nothing more was required.

Here, at Sully, just outside Bayeux, we began washing shirts and socks like mad, and bathing everybody from Montgomery downwards. In the intervals of washing, bathing, or performing other military functions we all settled to our several private hobbies. The suitably named L/Cpl. Smelt went fishing in the mill stream. Harry Noble and Johnnie Green and I went long walks, having first prudently learned in which direction lay the Germans. Goodness me, there was fighting within four miles of us, it was highly necessary to look out.

Bayeux itself I soon knew every stone of; it is a delightful city, not then however at its best. Practically the only things you could buy were picture postcards. I suppose I have more picture postcards of Bayeux than I shall ever use. That's why I am always so pleased to see those appeals which end, "Send a postcard to your M.P., NOW." And I do it.

At Sully I started a newspaper, *The Bubblers' Journal and Back Soapers' News*. Each morning I collected the B.B.C. news and passed on the nub to the rest of the unit; and to such villagers as could read English. These local worthies were somewhat puzzled by the rest of the paper's contents, particularly by the serial story, *The Sneezer's Prey*, which I think they read as news. Perhaps a few chapters of this fiction, which my colleagues flatteringly queued up to read, may be quoted here. It is rude, robust stuff. I have never secured a publisher for the finished work, but it's there if anybody wants it.

OUR GRIPPING NEW SERIAL STORY

THE SNEEZER'S PREY

An Adventure of Simon LeGrand
by Courtney Colleythorp

CHAPTER ONE

Curtains for Three

The slowly-moving Bentley glided to a stop. It was three o'clock. The mean Soho street gleamed in the wet moonlight.

Bambino's Club isn't easy to get into, especially at three o'clock, but Simon LeGrand made no bones about that. Leaping like a cat from the huge car, one heave of his 210 pounds of muscle and bone took him through the door and past the sleeping janitor. Coming up short, an automatic magically appeared in his hand, his steel-grey eyes took in the fantastic scene before him.

Bambino's is not a nice club; it smells of stale whisky and tobacco; through the haze a mixed company quarrelled and danced, and a few watched the tiny stage. Here a jaded pianist was playing, and before him a startlingly lovely naked girl was swaying her splendid hips in time with the music. Her heavy breasts leaned from her body like pears, her red lips invited. Simon LeGrand lighted a cigarette.

Unnoticed until now, as he moved the snub-nosed automatic gleamed menacingly in his hand and Jerry Mac the proprietor suddenly saw him, and cursed. With a sweep of his hand he put out the lights, amid cries and oaths. A bottle smashed. Amid the scuffling LeGrand inched himself forward, occasionally kicking a man's teeth in. He reached the stage door, and vanished. The club was now a roaring inferno. When the police arrived ten minutes later, LeGrand was gone, and so was the naked lady.

Forty miles away a reeking, roaring, streaming Bentley raged through the night, with a grim-faced man at the wheel and a naked woman in the back. First round to Simon LeGrand!

(Look out for tomorrow's gripping instalment!)

The fortunate reader of this book need not do that: for here it is:

THE SNEEZER'S PREY

CHAPTER TWO

The Sneezer Strikes

In the sombre house in St. John's Wood, the Sneezer sat smoking opium, idly running his hand through a heap of pearls. From the cellar, faintly, came the screams of a stool-pigeon undergoing torture, otherwise the house of mystery was as silent as the grave.

A soft buzz from the telephone. "Yes?"—"No.6 here. LeGrand has just cleaned up Bambino's and sloped with Lola Louse."

"Peste!"—for the Sneezer spoke perfect French—"Himmelkreuzerdonner wettersfuitenfelsnochmal!"—in perfect German, which he understood— "Ay de me!"—in fluent Spanish—and then, quietly, in English, he gave a few simple orders.

Two hundred miles away the Bentley slid to a stop at a level crossing. LeGrand was no longer in a hurry, otherwise he would have driven through it. A train rumbled past, and from the guard's van a grenade lobbed into the road; but LeGrand put a bullet into it in mid-air and the explosion hardly shook the car. The gates swung open and he drove steadily on.

But the lovely Lola Louse no longer lay naked in the back, and somewhere north of Ipswich, half turning, LeGrand met the little bloodshot eyes, and felt the stinking breath of a mad gorilla. LeGrand also knew French.

"Peste!" he said.

(See tomorrow's gripping instalment.)

I am inclined to think the next instalment cannot be printed but in order to reassure readers who fear the triumph of evil I will give the end of the story (adding in passing that the day we published a stop press announcement that Lola Louse had been discovered upside down in a dustbin in Dublin our French readers sent hourly messengers asking for the latest information).

THE SNEEZER'S PREY

CHAPTER TEN

Everybody Happy

The Sneezer crossed the road and entered the house. Behind him LeGrand disguised as a milkman, crept up the stairs. Yvonne answered the door and they entered. Lola lay on the bed covered (for the first time in this engaging history) with a counterpane. I hasten to add that every contour of her divine figure could clearly be seen through the clinging silk: not half.

It was time for a showdown. LeGrand stepped forward. "Lola!" he said —and her great hazel eyes opened—"Can I have your autograph?"

The Sneezer stepped between them. "This lady is my wife, and all matters relating to her go through me."

LeGrand accepted defeat. "May I have yours, then?" The great criminal signed his name on an old envelope and passed it to LeGrand. Picking his wife up, he carried her from the room. From the street a great roar was heard.

The Sneezer had stolen the Bentley.

But Simon LeGrand heard nothing; his eyes were on Yvonne.

"Will you come away with me, as soon as I can get another Bentley?" he said.

"Yes!" said Yvonne. "Wait while I take my clothes off . . ."

THE END

Of course, running a newspaper entails much more than merely finding a gripping serial. *The Bubblers' Journal* provided local news from the outside world; competitions; a radio guide; book reviews; and it was specially strong in its literary features, contributors including Matthew Prior, John Milton, G. Chaucer, John Dryden, Ernest Bramah and the authors of "Wit Restored". This kind of thing—contributed by Prior—opened the eyes of many chaps to the possibilities of the elder poets:

> Alas for my virginity—
> If I lose that (quoth Rose) I'll die!
> Behind the elms last night (said Dick)
> Rose, were you not extremely sick?

We were very lucky in our situation, about a quarter of a mile from the main road, for the full tide of the war passed us by. If one looked almost due north from the Mill, one saw a thick brown cloud hanging like a smoke screen over the fields where the road lay. This was the dust which for some sixteen hours daily had no chance to settle, for the traffic was quite literally nose to tail through there without a break all day— tank transporters, ration trucks, M.P's, units on the move, all the varied bustle of a quart army occupying a pint pot of land. Hundreds of men were actually living in this dust-cloud; eating, sleeping, working in it. They made excellent customers for the laundry.

Our men were living in tents in an orchard, but Harry Noble and I had a three-ton lorry backed up against the barn in which H.Q. office was located. In the upper floor of the barn lived a brood of sergeants, and above them was a corrugated iron roof. Harry and I could lie in bed and lob little stones on to this roof.

"Shrapnel was terrible last night," Sgt. B. used to report. It was said he slept in a tin helmet with another on his stomach. All the same, shrapnel is no joke and we did get our share of it. No doubt quite by chance there was a thick bundle of camouflage netting on the roof of the lorry, just over where I slept.

One evening about dusk we went up on to a bit of rising ground above the lane and watched the battle for Caen, a diabolical firework display. I made some verses about it and introduced them into a long poem I was writing—a long poem which was never finished, perhaps because no one set a time limit of fifteen minutes for its completion.

> Last night, after eleven, climbing the hill
> I stood watching the night-firing over Caen,
> A brilliant and uninterrupted prelude to the death of men,
> But the men standing by me, having no fear of death,
> Being here in no danger, jested, standing at ease;
> And I was half-ashamed to be with these
> Indifferent careless fellows that without quickened breath
> Such desperate beauty saw and honoured not;
> And I thought how having Betty by my side
> I might have comprehended these two certainties
> Of Death and Love now once before I died.
>
> Hand in hand there, on the edge of the wheat,
> Looking along the leagues of shattered sky
> To where the guns were laughing with red lips,
> To where the hell of man rushed up to meet
> The unimplicated heaven, I might try
> To understand, if Elizabeth were by.
>
> All night the guns replied their same reply.

However, I was never really at home with introspection and the like, despite my powerful aforementioned affinity with the metaphysicals. I preferred lyrics relating to kissing and such uncomplicated matters. All the same, with no immediate prospect of leave to encourage me, I did allow just a tincture of regret to creep into my work. "I have cried aloud the brevity of love", remarks (in Latin) one of the Latin poets. I was tempted to do the same.

Now to her body that with beauty bare
Lies in the burning sunshine of July
And can without a conscience offer there—
O God her body is beyond compare!—
The flower and sweet of love that does not die,

My verse I bring that chronicles her mood,
The way she rests her head, the way she will
With quiet limbs lie very lone and still—
O God she is with every grace endued!—
When love has loved his fill.

And I have seen her with retiring grace
Put her small slender hands upon her face—
O God such beauty in so little space!—
Her body that can banish where it lies
The heart-break from the shadows in my eyes—
O God there is no God if beauty dies!

See the World with a Mobile Laundry

From Sully we were ordered to Dieppe, a host of tanks and guns and bombers having thoughtfully preceded us to clear the way. I climbed in beside Corporal Naylor with lively anticipation. We were about to see a bit more of the world. And who better to see the world with than Jack? He never took both hands off the steering wheel while he turned round to abuse someone sitting behind And it was entirely through the aid of his green ink that I was able to put a few trees into my drawing of the Mill, Sully, which now hangs in the back kitchen. I'd like to see, incidentally, how far my murals have survived in that barn.

We joined the dust-cloud, now at last a little diminished for the seat of war was well over the horizon, and we trundled solemnly towards Dieppe. I was never happier than when the Laundry was on the move. There could hardly be any work for me since the office was all packed up in a three-ton lorry (about half of which consisted of my books and knick-knacks) and all I needed to do was enjoy the scenery and nod affably to such females under thirty as chanced to cross our path. Very few did; for as I have hinted, the mobile laundry in motion is a formidable sight. Down the long, straight, tree-lined roads we went, shocked and sobered by the destruction on every side. Some villages were completely demolished and the road went straight up and over the rubble like a switchback. Sometimes we drove for miles through the burnt-out shambles of a German column caught on the move and wiped out. Sometimes in an area almost clear of war's traces a single shattered tank would lie in the roadside ditch.

It was August—brilliant summer weather. I particularly

remember coming to a halt in a long avenue, cool and shady. One by one the lorries and trailers closed up behind us, and Cpl. R. got his stoves going. The great tins of corned beef were opened up. The biscuit and the tea and the pickles and the free cigarettes were set out and soon a dozen picnics were in progress. An officer moved from group to group with a vast biscuit and beef sandwich in his hand to let it be seen he was eating the same as the rest of us, before returning to his staff car to his real lunch. Occasionally along the road there passed some General, another mortal like ourselves with business far from the heat of battle. Overhead, lazily, a single aircraft circled: one of ours we all agreed, the single dissentient being Sgt. B. who believed it was a Messerschmidt.

Again, forty miles or so further on, we halted for tea beside a great empty farmhouse, with its courtyard embracing long, dark barns and brew houses and stables. Here were enormous wooden vats full of cider, which we were afraid to sample ("Sure to be poisoned!" said Sgt. B.); and in the walled garden, to which none but I penetrated (for most soldiers when not working go at once to sleep) I found several bunches of eatable grapes; and ate them. At last we drew up, as night began to fall, on the heights above Dieppe. Here in an orchard we found a German gun position, the guns still pointing along the road we had followed; but someone had taken the Germans away, and in fact they were in a cage nearby, with some ten thousand of their comrades. Which didn't satisfy Sgt. B., I'm afraid. Long after most of us had settled down he was peeping into dark corners, a lamp in one hand and a revolver in the other.

A Mobile Laundry needs lots of water; so does a Bath Unit. A good stream is fine, but a mill is better, for here usually there is a reserve of water, and a good depth. After a bit of scouting about the O.C. found a suitable site at Saqueville, about three miles outside Dieppe, and here we abode.

The laundry trailers contain powerful electric machinery of the latest type; two washers (rather like fish and chip ovens) and two driers; and of course generators, dynamos, pressure gauges, levers and wheels and every accessory. Thick, flexible pipes run hither and yon, on the one hand sucking in thousands of gallons of clean water and on the other putting out a similar quantity slightly soiled; cables quiver with the massive vibrations of the generators and the ceaseless throb of the machinery; the men tending the valves stand half-naked with the sweat gleaming on their bodies; the chaps on the washers push in hour after hour thousands of pairs of drawers, cellular, and hour after hour the chaps on the driers unhook them and fold them and bundle them and tie them. Everywhere there is the roar of steam and over all hangs a great white cloud. In all this ordered confusion the quiet word of Sgt. D. commands and controls.

In the next field stands an old shed which has been tastefully converted into a bathroom with a nice porcelain-enamelled bath, mats on the floor, hot pipes for towels and, I am sorry to learn afterwards, a concealed spyhole in the ceiling. Every afternoon the nurses from the hospital at Arques come in beautiful batches to bath.

They rank as Officers.

For the men there are showers behind a canvas screen, but we are not operating formally as a bath unit here, for there are few local troops and they have baths in Dieppe. We are washing the smalls of ten or fifty or two hundred thousand German prisoners in the cage up the road. Nobody knows how many there are, but anyhow they are more than enough to keep us busy.

"People are curious"—and here's an authentic instance. In all the weeks we were at Saqueville, from the middle of July until late autumn, one chap never had the curiosity to go into Dieppe and inspect the local amenities. He was cheerful, able-bodied, and indeed one of our best men. But when the day's work was over he retired to his bed and wrote to his wife and read a book until sleep overcame him. Every night a lorry went into the town carrying chaps to the theatre, the cafes, the cinema. Dieppe also had other attractions. But Pte. K. never once bothered.

But what a cheerful, lively, jolly little town it is. I used to wander with insatiable curiosity up and down its alleys, in and out of its churches. At week-ends, when a little more time could be taken I used to hitch-hike into Rouen, that wonderful old city. The destruction was lamentable, but how much loveliness remained! It is to be hoped that the municipality will provide, among the fine new buildings now in course of construction, a convenience for dames. Betty and I in the autumn of 1952 spent a profitless hour seeking something of the sort, and having little of the language were directed after every enquiry back to the statue of Joan of Arc. But we felt it was quite sufficient injury for the English to have burned the lady.

At Saqueville our men were accommodated for the first time under a solid roof; we occupied a fine chateau with towers at each corner, though not so fine a chateau as our neighbours a Pioneer unit had. Their home was the Chateau Miromesnil, Maupassant's birthplace. That was the kind of place to be born in, so long as the midwife had been sent for in good time: for it was a day's march to any outpost of civilization.

And then the day came when Pte. K. was forced, willy-nilly, to enter the town of Dieppe. We were on the road again, and our way lay down the long hill into the town and out the other side. Some hundreds of miles lay before us, and at the end the glittering city of Brussels. I was one of a small party sent on ahead to prepare the way. We crossed the battlefields of our fathers' war and paused at the summit of Hill 60 to admire that gaunt and impressive memorial. But to me more impressive were the trenches, still preserved, in which those thousands lived and died month after month, almost year after year, within hail of the enemy similarly living and dying across the way. That was the war of *Journey's End*. In Lille that night we had a glimpse of still more ancient conflicts, for we slept at a French Army barracks built (I should say) about the time of Louis XV and never modernised since. Nobody who spent a night there would ever be likely to join the Foreign Legion. Everything was made of stone, floors, walls, ceilings, stairs—beds, too, I fancy. It was damp and chilly, dark and hopeless. If there was any sanitation it was in the horses' department. Running water, none that we saw. Fires, none; though a good deal of smoke from somewhere.

But the next afternoon all was forgotten as we entered the streets of Brussels. Shops! Cafes! Girls! English girls, at that: A.T.S.! Beer! Cinemas! (Art galleries!—me, under my breath.)

Before sampling any or all of these delights, however, we wanted our tea.

A laundry site had been selected for us in a disused factory and to this we finally made our way. It was as dark and cheerless as a French Barracks, time of Louis XV. As we stood contemplating it the bitterest winter of the war set in. Our tea, and indeed all our meals until the laundry itself arrived, had to be taken with another unit at the other end of the city. So three times a day we huddled in our truck and drove through the freezing streets, arriving stiff and semi-conscious at the scene of breakfast, dinner, or what it was. We then took in as much food, as near boiling, as we could get. The return journey chilled us back again to the bone. I mention these melancholy details so that you will know that I, too, suffered for my country. I know everyone thinks mobile laundries were cushy. Alas, in general, I am happy to say they are quite right.

In Brussels apart from the attractions already noted there was music, hospitality, and indeed every virtue that ought to subsist in a nation's capital. I never wearied of the inexhaustible variety of this incomparable city. Standing on the level terrace by the Palace of Justice one could look down into the ancient city, not materially altered since the days of Breughel, whose bones still lie within a few yards of a market full of the bright, quarrelling, laughing crowds he loved.

For five or six months we enjoyed the best that Brussels could offer, and then once again the changing fortunes of war snatched

us up and deposited us in a damp field far from anywhere. This
was at Hees, Den., which (said Wilson Midgley) was not an
address at all. Well it was a large red brick mill somewhat
freely riddled with shell holes and standing a bare few yards
inside the German border, with Holland over the way. Our
playground now was Nijmegen, to be reached twice a week by
unit transport. As we entered Germany for the first time we
were confronted by large notices, "THIS IS ENEMY TERRITORY",
etc., and I fancy we all huddled a little closer together. From
now on, we thought, every man's hand is against us. Nothing of
the kind. Before we had been two days in Hees, Den., a large
consignment of German girls was delivered to us. These were
to learn the business of washing. (Of course, at Brussels we had
employed civilian labour, too. But here in the heart of the
fields the affair took on another complexion.) I have no idea
how much the girls learned about washing, but I do know we
took occasion to publish daily in Part I Orders the instruction
that fraternising was forbidden. You tell that to a laundryman
decently lost with a German girl in a woolly cloud of steam.

How they smiled and chattered and enjoyed being washer-
women, those girls.

A mysterious old man used to make himself available for the
vending of schnapps, a colourless liquid which I for one looked
at askance. On every blank wall were the sinister posters
advertising the werewolves, those German undercover men
who would stick at nothing, we were told. Achtung! 'ware
schnapps, we said to one another. A bottle of it which I took
home once on leave we used, one spoonful at a time, to light
the fire with. It was also an efficient paint remover. But we did
get a supply of magnificent Dutch gin, from official sources. Of
course, I wasn't high enough up, as a lance-corporal, to be
trusted with spirits. But all the same I never went short.

I first encountered the quaint custom of denying spirits to any
soldier under the rank of Sergeant at Normanton Barracks
when I joined up. At a social the officers and senior N.C.O's
had a bar of their own in the corner, with a variety of choice

drinks, cigarettes, etc. We men had a barrel of beer in the
other corner, take it or leave it. Now, you know, it is rather
absurd, this business of rank. Let's have rank, by all means.
In fact I have determined to be a Lieut.-Colonel myself next
time. But don't let's make complete idiots of ourselves with
stupidities like this one about whisky being for people who can
be trusted not to go berserk after one or two tots and murder
the R.S.M. I suppose the real answer is that there wouldn't be
enough for the officers if we let supplies go to the men. But that's
a naive suggestion: for when did the officers go short of anything
merely to avoid inconvenience to the men? You will pardon this
small aside. Of the forty or fifty officers with whom I came into
close contact, a mere half-dozen commanded and deserved
respect. With the rest it was a question of every man for
himself, using every advantage of rank, privilege and position.
Kindly turn to Appendix A if you wish to pursue this topic
further.

From Hees, Den., we moved in due course to Schloss Wissen,
Weeze, in the Rhineland. Our nearest centre was Goch, but a
mobile cinema once a week there or at Kavelar was about the
limit of entertainment resources in those parts. You had to
make your own entertainment. This Harry Noble, Johnnie
Green and I very well knew how to do, for the castle provided
all sorts of interesting facilities.

To begin with, it had a moat, an extensive waterway with
various ramifications, fed by the main river at the end of the
grounds. The castle proper was entirely surrounded by water,
and the gardens were again surrounded beyond the inner
channel. And what gardens! All tangled now, but formerly
a splendid domain with walks and arbours and hot houses and
prospects and naked ladies made of marble and urns and
gazebos and exotic trees and shrubs. Beyond these gardens lay
orchards and kitchen gardens and pastureland. Here (and we
arrived at the right time of the year) were currants and straw-
berries and apples and pears and peaches and plums. Vegetables too, any amount of them.

The castle was entered by way of a fine bridge and under an arch in which were still to be seen the relics of drawbridge and portcullis. The H.Q. office was here, in what must formerly have been the guard room.

Harry and I slept in a modern wing (mid-seventeenth century, I should say). In the main castle there were no troops sleeping, but the great hall made a pleasant canteen and would also accommodate a cinema show. Generally speaking, we were not encouraged to explore the castle beyond those parts in our occupation; but I never really understood the orders I issued (under general advice from the O.C.) to be intended for my own use as well. Anyhow, Harry and I investigated every nook of the place. It was a fine affair.

We had a couple of rowing boats on the moat and would lazily paddle about or just lie drifting. When this seemed too tame we would go on the river which was wide and deep and swiftly flowing. There were quite a lot of boats. Here and there a solitary soul would go easily along, but usually eight or ten chaps would crowd into one boat, all pulling lustily, and these heavily freighted vessels would drive through the water like express trains, scattering all before them amid confident cries from the mariners, and shrieks of despair from persons venturing to go for a bathe. At one cottage about a mile downstream (said rumour) it was proper to land and frat. But these pieces of intelligence always came my way a month or so after we had moved elsewhere.

Back on the Bottom Rung

Most of the time now the four Bath Sections were detached and having a wonderful time. They each consisted of a Sergeant and three men, with one lorry, and they used to camp by a stream or other water supply and set up in business to serve local troops. I can think of few people better able to attend to their own comfort that an R.A.O.C. Bath Section: unless indeed it be the L/Cpl. clerk of a Mobile Laundry.

The pastoral life at Weeze came to an end, but not before I had met Alan Powell walking casually across the bridge into the castle as though the fact that we hadn't met for five years meant nothing; which indeed it didn't, seeing that he was merely calling to ask the way and had no notion that I was there.

At that time we were a mere twenty miles or so inside Germany, but the next move took us nearly to Hanover. G.H.Q. 21 Army Group had now shifted from Brussels to Bad Oeynhausen and we were to join it once more. This meant reunion with certain A.T.S. girls, for those who enjoyed taking up again threads formerly laid down; and the chance to form new friendships for the rest. Some chaps did both.

Life in Bad Oeynhausen was odd. The whole town had been cleared of civilians and surrounded by barbed wire, etc. And then the H.Q. moved in. The laundry was in a corner of the town near the wire, and looked out into open country. The Germans were apt to laugh at us; it certainly looked as if we were the conquered. The town was not unattractive in a heavy, German sort of way. The baths, kurhaus, theatre, etc., were dotted about in a large park and were very soon turned into E.N.S.A. and N.A.A.F.I. establishments. The baths themselves were an improvement on our Bath Sections, and among other refinements there was a corps of old men whose business apparently was to scrub backs.

Another interlude came—I think probably before the Bad Oeynhausen move—when the laundry was ordered to pack up and return to England. The Bath Sections were to remain in Germany. This splitting of the unit left one officer and me as "H.Q.", and the four sections. We were attached to an R.S.D. at Dusseldorf. Pray don't ask what an R.S.D. was; I count myself fortunate in not knowing.

At Dusseldorf life was entirely and wholly blissful. I did no work at all, beyond issuing orders to the officer each morning. It was here that I copied out the entire poetical works of E. H. Visiak with a view to their eventual publication in a single volume. I engaged in several other literary enterprises. I was also reunited to Christopher Dilke (as he then was[1]). Christopher was now a Lieut.-Colonel and in Brussels he had been merely a major—though a particularly impressive one. I had met him (I think) through Jaspar Sayer; and I had met *him* through my Brussels publisher, Albert de Visscher. Anyway, Christopher was now running a fine newspaper and we conspired to get me posted to it, but alas jealousy in high places intervened. It was at Dusseldorf that I received a flattering request from C. Dilke: would I write three poems to stand one each at the head of the three sections of his new novel?

Something went wrong with this assignment. I wrote one poem and passed it to my patron for approval and somehow the other two didn't get any further. In the end Christopher gracefully solved the whole dilemma by dedicating one third share of the book to me and using a phrase from the poem for his title. Here's the whole thing:

FRANCE, 1940
France is a star! such nations fashion Fate,
And this, that gave a name to Liberty,
Now holds herself aloof from infamy

[1] And still is.

13

And—hardly conquered—steels herself to wait
The turning wheel's return to lovely ways;
Now sadly but with springing hope her eyes
Follow the battles in the northern skies;
Look inward, France, with the same searching gaze
That now you scan the lean horizon there
Along the Channel and the English air,
For what within you failed the trusting State,
That in the unaccustomed dust there lies
By war's ill-chance and Frenchmen's treacheries
What once before the world was proud and great.

I copy the poem here for two reasons. First, because it pleased Arthur Ball who, like the gentleman in *Hudibras*, knows what's what, and can also read Chaucer in the original; and next because when it was formerly printed I overlooked two misprints which still further increased the poem's essential obscurity.

Just as we were reconciled to our new life the word came to join up again with the Laundry, which hadn't gone to England after all. I packed all up and let the officer understand that this move wasn't to affect my leave. I could find my way back afterwards to the new location and even without my help he ought to be able to take four lorries and four generators to wherever it was they had to go. Glumly, he agreed.

But where were they to go? This was not clear; the latest place known to me was Lubecke and accordingly on my return from leave I proceeded there, only to be laughed to scorn by the troops in that sloping city. They hadn't had any clean linen for weeks and they bathed under the tap if at all. Two or three days I wandered up and down Germany calling softly under my breath so as not to arouse suspicion, "Wiggy? Wilkie? Harry Noble . . .?"

And, now I come to think of it, it was at Bad Oeynhausen that I ran them to earth. Harry, Jack Naylor and I had a house to ourselves just outside H.Q. office, which was in the administrative block of a small factory or stock yard. That was an astonishing little house. It had begun, I think, as a farm. It had big kitchens, etc., and small living-rooms, the whole affair obviously of great age. Across the way in a much bigger and altogether better house lived a bunch of A.T.S. girls, but I had no friends among them. At Brussels I had become friendly with one or two girls who attended discussions, etc., at the Study Centre and this establishment, under my droll friend Rigby, was now in Bad Oeynhausen; but the girls were in the next town—I forget its name. So most evenings we had to talk about poetry without any female pipings. One girl whom I knew slightly did on one occasion come up, riding a horse, and demand audience with me. I am afraid of horses.

The war was nearly over, obviously: for I was now promoted acting-corporal. A good deal of the office work consisted of working out details about getting demobbed. A number of well-known characters departed, never to return, each carrying a packet of sandwiches and much more kit than you would think one man could require. One hopeful is said to have taken home a wardrobe in sections. Most were weighed down with extra sets of vests, winter woollens, and drawers, cellular. By the way, those string vests they used to issue for Arctic wear are awfully good and quite easily unravelled; they make a ball of strong string which would cost about four shillings in the shops.

At last my turn came. The first stage of the trip terminated at Tournai and I found occasion to inspect the cathedral, the only one I ever saw with five towers. The barracks at Tournai was like the one at Lille, but the fact that we were on our way home helped a little, and anyway we were there only one night. Next day we arrived at the familiar transit camp at Calais. It was in the streets of Calais one morning about seven thirty, as I was stretching my legs before catching the leave boat, that I was stopped by a Canadian soldier: "Say, where do you get a woman in this town?" I had no idea, but I directed him to what I took to be the cathedral, quite unmaliciously. Social life in many cities has its roots in the church.

Calais-Dover; Dover-York. Here they first began calling us Mister. We were issued with extra chocolate ("Catching votes!" hissed the man in front, whom I judged to be expert in the political set-up). And of course, civilian suits, etc. I chose a natty grey which I subsequently sold for £1 because when I got it home it unaccountably didn't fit. The mackintosh I still use to go out in wet nights and fill the coal buckets. All this and other spoil was packed into a cardboard box rather like the ones we used to carry our gas-masks in, only a bit bigger, and me and it and several parcels of drink, loot, extra underwear, etc., were placed in a train for Sheffield.

Yes, Sheffield again, an essential link in the chain that connects York with Derby. So far as the military authorities were concerned, I was now free to take up my career where I laid it down. If I wanted to go on being a Poet, third class, it was my affair. The honourable trade of Clerk (Regimental) Second Class could be set aside for ever. But I had better look out! Somewhere in the papers about my release it said in very small type that they could get me back any time they wanted. I fancy it also said you hadn't got to mess up your uniform. Charlie went down the pit in mine.

My Gratuity was £36—I may be tuppence out one way or the other. I know that they announced in Parliament that these sums were to enable people to set up in business, etc. So I was careful not to spend mine at first, although it would have been handy. Instead I went along to one of the organisations that exists to give comfort and advice to soldiers. Would their terms of reference (I enquired) allow them to give me assistance to transport my household goods back to London, where my work was. Certainly not! (I was an acting corporal, wasn't I? Well then.) What was my Gratuity for? The few poor thousands of pounds they had at their disposal were needed for Sergeant Majors. And that is the sober reason why I never set up in business like they said in Parliament.

Before we could return to London we had to find accommodation, and at that time, mid-1946, the task was mighty formidable. Mrs. Adam came to the rescue (as she does in almost any situation, given the chance) and put us up in the blue room while we tramped the streets looking for places to let. At last we found a place in West Hampstead which we could have in exchange for housework. Betty nobly undertook to do this and we moved in, privately determined to get something more suitable when occasion served. This determination did our hosts no disservice: for Betty scrubbed and dusted to perfection for about six months and when we finally moved she left the house gleaming like a new pin.

Unestablished Author

It was delightful to be together again after that tedious separation, and a wonderful thing to be back in London. We were poor, but not quite so poor as formerly and the author of two books can hold up his head in any literary company (not that I mixed in much, anyway). So far as I could see the way was now clear to go ahead and be famous.

I proceeded to write a book that sold some sixty thousand copies. What! (the reader cries) did fame come so easily as that? Well, no. . . .

Eric Warman was actively engaged at this time in publishing the Books of the Film. These were short novels based on successful films, written and published by arrangement with the film companies. They were attractively produced, fully illustrated, and priced at two shillings. I should think several millions of copies were sold in those years immediately following the war.

Into this thriving concern I was received to assist Eric as a sort of secretary: I was a confidential private secretary of the most advanced kind: I knew such things as the kind of straw- berry jam to order, and what to say to the laundry when it sent back a shirt lamentably marked with somebody else's name. I also accompanied Eric to the studios, standing always a little behind him like I had seen bodyguards do on the films. Occasionally I spoke to people like Greta Gynt and Paula Valenska and David Tomlinson. I have drunk gin with Michael Wilding when he had nothing on but a dressing gown! And of course producers, directors, camera and publicity men I called by their first names (when these were known to me).

And in the end I was promoted to writing Books of the Film.

A Book of the Film took nine days to write, on average. This was thirty thousand words, say four thousand a day if you leave out the week-end. Eric, who could always do everything more efficiently than me, once wrote one in three days; perhaps I had better not say which one.

The work always followed a fairly set formula. First of all, one saw the completed film, usually at the studio: for of course at this stage it had not been released to the picturegoer. Then with the film itself clear in mind one sat down with a copy of the shooting script, which supplied the whole dialogue and certain stage directions, etc. And with this at one's elbow the book soon got written. It is commonly said that the film isn't a bit like the book; the boot now was on the other foot, at least as far as my works were concerned: the book wasn't always very like the film. Take *Vice Versa*, for example. Peter Ustinov had great fun with Anstey's book and made a delightful film. Along I came and turned the whole thing back into a book, here and there modifying the film script and here and there giving something suspiciously reminiscent of Anstey—but not very often. I have always said anyone who has seen the film should read the book. My book.

I say "my book", but you'll have to take my word for it. To my great grief, Books of the Film were all written under a set of pseudonyms used jointly by our great team of writers. One of these, D. L. Ames, was allowed to use his own name, but not we others. I was usually Warwick Mannon (but collectors are requested to note that not all books by this author are by me), but once I was Arnold Meredith. Why these two great Victorian names were thus linked to make a filmwriter's holiday I never learned. My most successful work was *Spring in Park Lane*, of which the public with fine discrimination consumed well over a hundred and twenty thousand copies.

Now, if I say I used to knock off my four thousand words before going to the office, do not think that I am claiming some merit comparable with that usually accorded to Trollope. I mention it because perhaps one or two of my readers who are setting forth to be writers may profit from the tip—a tip by no means new. Indeed, it was reaffirmed to me only a month ago by Monk Gibbon. It is, simply, that the mere mechanical part of writing a book consists in *sitting down and getting on with it.* Don't be misled by the geniuses who polish and repolish and never attain the haven of their desires. These worthies are of two sorts: those with a natural aptitude for fine writing, which is excellent if you are born with it; and those who attain to excellence by constant practice and revision. If you come into the first class, I need say no more. But if you don't, don't ally yourself to the second unless you have a private income. The best way to become a writer is to sit down and write. Above all, I think it is essential to accustom oneself to composing straight on to the typewriter, and get it right first time. Those Books of the Film were useful training: they went straight from the typewriter to the printer without any more revision than the odd word here and there, and they were all the better for it.

After a while I added a third job to the others. Before breakfast I was the successful novelist; in mid-morning I was the efficient private secretary; after lunch I went along and did cataloguing for Bertram Rota. All really keen collectors of Hopkins should note that I wrote the anonymous preface to Mr. Rota's Catalogue No. 75. This (oddly enough) was the first bookseller's catalogue in which my own works figured. For *Love and Elizabeth*, I notice, Mr. Rota demanded six shillings. For *Miscellany Poems* he was content to receive a mere two—perhaps even at this price the work was unsaleable. In 1954 the price of *Love and Elizabeth* had appreciated to seven and six—but that was a copy inscribed by the author.

Love and Elizabeth is not commonly met with in the shops, although for a book of poems it sold pretty well. I expect the original purchasers prefer to keep it always to hand. Anyhow, I have only once or twice come across second-hand copies—and I always look on the poetry shelves under H where they are classified, and for a rather thin blue book in a white jacket if they are higgledy-piggeldy. However, I did come across a copy not long ago in Chancery Lane for a shilling. Now, as I have already given a copy of this book to practically everyone I know, I had no immediate need for another. And I spent my shilling on something else. But furtively, in the basement, unobserved, I wrote in that copy against "is."—"and worth every penny of it. Kenneth Hopkins." This good deed done, I shuffled off.

So when Bertram catalogued an inscribed copy I went along to see which of the people to whom I had given one had thus basely hastened to sell it. But it was none of them: it was my Chancery Lane copy, much mutilated by the rubbing out of that necessary "is." without which the inscription was meaningless. So I commanded them to put it back, even if they were proposing to charge seven and six. The only other copy anybody ever asked seven and six for (so far as my extensive researches go) was the copy I gave to Gilbert Frankau. Frankau, like many other popular writers, was a much more respectable figure in letters than the critics make out. Several of his books are first-class by any standards. On the few occasions that we met he was unfailingly friendly to me, but he caused me a good deal of amusement once at the Cavalry Club. I suppose I am the only acting corporal ever to have been entertained to tea there. All through tea Frankau kept bobbing up as various aged members hobbled past with: "Evening, General!", "Evening, Colonel!", "Hi there, Field Marshal!!—Bridge tonight?" and these relics of the Crimea would issue toothless greetings and pass on. Luckily my demob suit concealed the fact that I had been little more than a camp follower in the late dreadful conflict.

Of course one of our first ports of call on returning to London was the Saturdays, now a firmly established society busily writing books of unalterable greyness. I am afraid Persis found my grey books a disappointment: she may have thought I wasn't trying because when most people (like the character in Flecker's poem) "did not shrink from sentiment" and wrote "serious" poems, mine were usually flippant. Mine and R. P. Lister's—

but then Richard was a funny man anyway. But I wrote Sonnets! and should know better.

The Saturdays were fortunate in possessing several remarkable members who would have been outstanding figures in any company. Of these was Vivian Locke Ellis. V. was as much the complete poet in his own way as was Arnold Vincent Bowen in his. V. was the "up-in-the-clouds" poet of fiction: impracticable, absent-minded, other-worldly. He once had a window from which he couldn't see the garden, so he elevated two or three flowers in pots on stilts to the necessary height—twenty feet or so—to provide a suitable view. Only a lesser man would have thought of a window box. Of course he composed poems on the backs of letters about to be posted to remote parts of the world, and left to himself would live on bread and tea, or forget to eat at all. He was full of stories of a generation most of us were too young to remember, going back to the days of King Edward, when people like Rupert Brooke and Wilfrid Gibson and de la Mare were the coming men. Between V. and Arnold Bowen there was an immediate bond: each recognised a considerable poet in the other. It was in 1947 that the Saturdays celebrated the publication of V's *Collected Poems*, a book full of astonishing beauties and marked throughout by the writer's rare personality.

Another Saturday was Cora J. Gordon—Jo. A paragraph cannot hope to do justice—indeed, a whole book could not do justice to Jo. She was unique, and irreplaceable.

Usually, Jo arrived a little late, but not unannounced. Foreknowledge of her imminent arrival was carried to the ears above, even in the midst of a general buzz of talk, by a clatter on the stairs and the reassuring cry, "It's only me!" The clatter would be caused by Jo tripping over one of her carpet bags, or getting one of her ropes of beads hitched up on the doorknob as she entered—which would set the bell jangling. For Jo was apt to wear and carry extraordinary things, collected for the most part in remote corners of Europe and never finally discarded. "What a delightful scarf, Jo!" one would say. "Yes, isn't it," she would answer, "it's an Albanian peasant's Sunday stocking. They weave them from goat combings and briza-grass. We had one for a sling when Jan broke his leg on Baba Krch, and I brought along the other. After all, the girl couldn't go to church in odd stockings, could she, and it would be absurd to wear only one." Or perhaps one would remark on Jo's attractive handbag and she would admit it was a Lap-lander's skull cap, really; her shoes were bought in Portugal, her skirt was Dutch, her beads, native work from Cyprus.

Bright-eyed, quick-fingered, Jo would sit in a corner sketching and every now and then some extraordinary anecdote would fall into the conversation. There was no need to hear the beginning or the end to enjoy the flavour of these traveller's tales, for they always went with a bang all through. "I remember we were travelling in the Blue Train once with a mongoose on the rack . . ." or, ". . . so we had to bring the mummy through the Customs full of this gin . . ."

Jan and Jo Gordon wrote a dozen highly entertaining travel books, but Jo always seemed to have a few adventures left over that hadn't got into the books. Her flat was like herself, full of wonders. It was a large ground-floor and basement in Notting Hill. Every room was stacked with paintings and sketches and with chests of drawers overflowing with paints, pencils, crayons, curios, letters, drawings, hairpins from Montenegro, queer-shaped bottles, bits of native cloth and everything else. On the walls by ends of string hung all kinds of musical instruments, mainly stringed, and Jo, plucking a note or two, would say, "This is a *bania* from Guinea, jointed with human blood to give it a better tone—ping! pretty, isn't it?" Even eating a simple snack at Jo's was an adventure; the dainties were apt to be from the wildest regions of Soho and prepared according to the method perfected by the Serbs before that nation was converted to Christianity in A.D. 301. "Try this, it's delicious, I learnt how to do it in Kracow!" would be the invitation to a dish at once black and angry, with things *heaving* in it, and only fingers to serve it with.

Perhaps I exaggerate a little; but normal-size treatment wouldn't be any good with Jo. Her death was as gallant as her life. She died making plans till the last and protesting that a silly bit of pain was teasing rather than actively troublesome.

It was at the Saturdays that I developed the habit (and I think it is a good one) of writing shorter and shorter poems. Sometimes the poem was short, anyway; at other times it was long and I prudently suppressed the greater part of it. These two lines seem to me complete in themselves, although they were originally accompanied by others:

> A Garden is a loathsome thing, God wot,
> And some like gardening, but I do not.

Of course, Oswell Blakeston has carried this search for the perfection of brevity much further. His *Poems*, *A Single Word* (One Word World Publications. 1 pistole.) was a singular contribution to the study which has not had the influence it deserves, perhaps because the edition was only one copy. I venture to quote a complete poem:

> Cresive

which I singled out for special praise when I reviewed the book in the *Town Crier*. I was never able to write any effective poem under two lines, unless you admit the following (which, however, doesn't rhyme):

> Gentleman John, the Judas of Fleet Street

Another rather short work which, however, contains an undoubted truth, was "A Conversationalist":

> When Hop
> Comes to a stop
> Kins
> Begins.

As a matter of fact, I am not quite so tireless a talker as that, because I long ago learned that the best conversation is give-and-take, and I have been lucky enough to hear the other side of the question from a host of eloquent masters.

When our sojourn at West Hampstead came to an end we

entered upon one of the most remarkable tenancies of our life, in a basement flat at Alexander Street, W.2. This is a jolly backwater of Bayswater, tucked away behind Westbourne Grove. A row of tall Victorian houses, now in somewhat reduced circumstances; a group of little shops; a pleasant pub; and comparative peace, because the traffic seldom ventures into what is virtually a cul-de-sac. I say "comparative peace" because at night the neighbourhood was apt to wake up. Screams and cries of "Murder" were not uncommon after twelve and dreadful unexplained bumps and thuds went on until two or three in the morning.

Our basement had formerly been occupied by a mad artist if one may judge by the evidence left on the walls: bits of imitation masonry, fragments of stained glass, shelves balanced in dark corners, and a taste for paint in violent primary colours characterised his ideas of interior decoration. However, we weren't there long enough for the surroundings to become a real burden.

Less easily to be tolerated were two other local features: an army of slugs which appeared at night and took general possession, retiring undefeated into various cracks in the morning; and a dampness so utter that if a room was left undisturbed for a day or so it was almost necessary to paddle on next entering it. A green mould quickly grew on most of our possessions, the straw seats of chairs began to sprout and the smell of wet surge continued to hover about us even after an hour or two in the warm sunshine. My typewriter went rusty.

I don't know how long we would have endured these inconveniences in order to continue enjoying having a pub more or less next door. It was quite a different thing that finally determined us to look for a home elsewhere. One day with no other warning than a loud creak the ceiling of our bathroom came down, bringing with it the bath in the room above. This incident was occasioned by dry rot, which was apparently having a field day in the upper floors. Two baths (one suspended drunkenly over the other) were more than we could effectively use and although the landlord made light of the incident (he lived somewhere else) we never again felt wholly comfortable there. Betty by superhuman efforts and the expenditure of £200 secured a flat off Ladbroke Grove and once more the books, the knicks and the knacks were severally transported.

For the first time in my life I was now able to have a study. How often had I gazed in envy at the pictures of authors sitting at ease, pen in hand, looking across spacious rooms, through windows opening upon smooth lawns, to the infinite blue-cloaked hills. "Sir Edmund Gosse in his Study." "Mr. Silas K. Hocking in his Study." "Mr. A. C. Swinburne in his Study." Sometimes it was a Library; but I think only the editor of *The Magnet* had a Den.

My study looked straight down the street opposite and gave a small but recurring glimpse of the trains of the District line dashing to and fro between Hammersmith and Ladbroke Grove by way of Latimer Road. Here were composed several Books of the Film and I know not how many sonnets. No more flimsy tables set in basement windows with work inevitably distracted by ankles passing above. No more clearing away, even with a sentence still on the stocks, in order to lay the cloth for supper. Step by step I was becoming an author like real authors.

The new flat was a fair size and soon made a port of call for all sorts of itinerant passengers. Practically everyone we knew outside London found it impossible to go to Switzerland or Italy or Australia without spending a night or so with us en route. I soon had by heart the times of trains and ships to all parts. We were as handy for Tilbury as for Victoria and once, I think, made the perfect jumping off place for a party of nine bent on embarking at Immingham.

It was one of our visitors who displayed a lamentable lack of the proper respect that ought to be paid to an Author's Study. One morning as I was sitting down at my desk to commence the day's operations I noticed neatly piled beside my typewriter, and established on the first draft of a sonnet that lay there, a small pile of toenail parings. Our only guest at this time was a Colonial writer and when I drew his attention to these relics, asking with pardonable sarcasm if he had finished with them, he complained bitterly that my scissors were blunt. However he was not perhaps quite so difficult a guest as the one returning to some northern outpost on Easter Sunday who insisted on taking our last crust of bread to sustain him during the journey.

We also occasionally had a lodger or so. There was the girl whom we took in, at the urgent request of a certain poet, because he wanted to live with her husband. This girl thought the room, the rent, everything, entirely suitable. A few minutes after she took up her tenancy Betty made a cup of tea and thought it would be friendly to offer one to the lodger. But the lodger was already in bed and fast asleep (it was about four in the afternoon). At eleven or thereabouts she dressed and went out. We saw her at odd moments about twice a week and learned that her boy friend was planning to move in because she found the walk to his garret in Holborn a bit much. We couldn't, however, allow this to happen for fear of shocking great-grandfather across the landing; for he had already begun to form the habit of coming down off the wall.

We enjoyed some lively conversation in that Ladbroke Grove flat. Looking through our visitors' book I find, among others, the names of Hesketh Pearson, John Redwood Anderson, H. Pearl Adam, Eileen Bigland, Meum Stewart, Alice and Christopher Dilke, Anna and John Boylan, Anna and Arthur Ball, Clifford Bax, John Waller, William Kean Seymour, Wilfrid Gibson, Edmund Blunden, Beresford Egan and Louis Marlow. Some good talk there!

For a time during our years at Ladbroke Grove, Louis Marlow had no London flat and he was a fairly frequent visitor when in town. I think he and Clifford Bax are the two outstanding examples of what I conceive to be the eighteenth-century manner that I have met—and also Algernon Cecil, whom I knew only slightly. The characteristics I have in mind are a courtesy wholly alien to our unlettered day, an appreciation of literature, art, and wine inherent rather than acquired. A deference and consideration towards women which (generally speaking) women themselves have elsewhere destroyed. And an awareness of life's goodness if temperately savoured, and not greedily snatched. There is much to be learned from such men; but alas, too few of them from whom to learn it.

With a settled and final home in London and a sufficient if not spectacular income to maintain it, I was able now to go quietly forward with my lesser enterprises. It was not necessary for every effort to be directed solely towards filling purse and mouth. But just in case there might be a failing demand for Books of the Film when I came to the age of sixty and seventy I kept in touch with other branches of literature. I contributed more or less regularly to a number of journals—*Time and Tide*, *Punch*, *Lilliput*, *John o' London's Weekly*, *The Spectator*, *World Review* and so on. I did a fair amount of film journalism, too.

And I had a sonnet broadcast to North Africa.

General Character and Disgusting Habits

Most autobiographies turn out to be not what the writer was like, but what happened to him. In an attempt to avoid this defect (for so I esteem it) I will now get together a few notes about myself as a person, taking no account of any influence I may have exerted in the framing of a Peace Treaty with Japan.

Certainly one of my most disgusting habits is the way I eat sweet pickle, chutney, various sauces (including one which is said by the makers to be "piquant and appetising") *and even beetroot*. This is what I do: I get a large lump of cheese and two or three thick slices of bread on one plate—sometimes I tear the greater part of a loaf to pieces with my bare hands instead of cutting it. Then on another plate, or as likely as not, a saucer, I pour out perhaps three fluid ounces of the sauce, or about six square inches (cubic square inches, that is) of the pickle, or *beetroot in proportion*. I am now ready to take my supper (for this type of repast does not appeal at breakfast time).

It will be noticed that so far I have no knife and fork, those conventional refinements.

So I break off two pieces of bread a couple of inches square, and using them as gardeners in the park use two flat boards to scoop up a pile of dead leaves, I scoop up a generous measure of pickle and convey it to my mouth. All the time, of course, I am reading Thurber, or *Pickwick*, or Saintsbury's *History of English Prose Rhythm*. Now and again I take a mouthful of cheese, or a long pull at a pint of cold water.

Can you wonder that Betty sometimes says, "I can't think why I married you?"

Sometimes she says to me, "Don't eat so fast." I don't eat anything like so fast as John Symonds. When we used to go to tea with him at Hill Road he always divided the available food equally into three portions and before we could politely fall to he would have finished his share and be looking with interest at ours. I remember once (after we had both advanced in the world to a temporary prosperity) he and I lunched together in a Chinese restaurant in Soho. The place was not crowded, and there were no appreciable delays in the service. We ate straight through one of those enormous meals they serve if one doesn't take care to specify that enough food for sixteen is not required, and we had paid the bill and were out in the street within fifteen minutes.

At other times Betty says to me, "This is you." She then hunches herself up until her nose nearly touches her plate, holds knife and fork in tightly clenched fists, allows her hair to fall grotesquely over her eyes, and begins to make odd sucking noises. Then I know she is mocking me, and I chew the next mouthful forty times. I spent too much time in my youth letting food get cold while I watched to see which fork people picked up ever to be at a loss now in any company. The only time I was left with no defence happened once at Bath, and will form a paragraph in the next volume of my memoirs.

But I must particularly protest at the sucking noises Betty makes when she mocks me. After all, the only way to find out if a cup of tea is too hot is to keep well away from it and take a very small sip. If at the same time the little finger is kept crooked away from the handle of the cup, which is delicately gripped by first finger and thumb only, the appearance of confident gentility in the gesture will to a large extent offset the admitted vulgarity of the sucking noise which inevitably accompanies the sip.

This is altogether better than taking a great gulp and then having to rush out with eyes popping and face red to get a drink of cold water at the tap. Neither do I recommend Aunt Eff's practice of adding cold water to the tea—not to her own tea, for she was grown up and able to cope, but to mine when I was seven and unable (as I affirmed) to wait while it got cool.

I always wear my hair too long. I have it cut about five times a year, and never until we have had words about it more than once. But in this matter I will certainly defend myself. I have quite nice hair and the longer it gets the more it curls. It curls up at the back in really quite an attractive way, and in conjunction with my extraordinary moustache gives me an appearance at once distinctive and sinister. Sir Jacob Epstein once said to me, "What have you got yourself up to look like Balzac for?" and others have noticed a resemblance to R. L. Stevenson, Andrew Lang (the picture where he's sitting in a chair apparently in either the last stages of exhaustion or the first of *rigor mortis*) and Sir Philip Sidney. I let them rail; at least my moustache saves me from being called Madam by bus conductors, which used occasionally to happen before I had it.

Many of the unpleasant things about me I have heard from my wife. One of the first things I do at night when I get home is take off my tie which (it seems) I then let fall wherever I chance to be. So the house is littered with ties, for I wear a different one most days. Some of these ties formerly belonged to Aleister Crowley, including one which in the end I gave to Ronnie Laws. This specimen was covered with magical symbols and I was afraid to wear it lest it strangled me.

I was one of the "long-haired devotees" described in the press as present at Crowley's funeral. In fact I had the longest hair of them all. But I wasn't technically a devotee. I simply wanted to hear Louis Marlow read Crowley's *Hymn to Pan*, which he did superbly. The wild and barbaric words echoed round the Crematorium, "Io, Pan! Pan!" until I for one expected that ancient God to rise up through the floor. Afterwards we walked back into Brighton and Gerald Yorke gently pulled the reporters' legs. "Mr. Yorke, did you ever actually see Mr. Crowley perform magic?" "Oh, yes, countless times!" "What did he do?" "Oh, well, he was very fond of turning himself into a pillar of salt." Crowley got a very good press for his obsequies.

I not only never put my ties away, but I always have to be

reminded to change my socks; and another thing I never do until driven to it is get my shoes mended.

In washing up (I usually do the wiping, because *I don't wash clean*) I always pick up and wipe the last thing washed and put down, so that at the bottom of the pile there are cups and saucers that don't get wiped until they are dry anyway. Betty is continually snatching a dripping soup plate from my hands and pressing into them instead a well-drained pudding basin. But I never really learn this lesson, and that's why I prefer washing and wiping on my own. Then, too, there is the vexed question of whether or not you need soap powder and soda. And is it in fact safe now, in these days of greater scientific progress, to let the handles of knives get wet?

Another of my worst habits, and one which has persisted from early youth, is putting things off. I will justify this habit some other time.

My wife has a disconcerting way of saying about three o'clock in the afternoon (if it's a week-end) or soon after I get home at night (if it's a week day), "You know you haven't cleaned your teeth, don't you?"

"Yes I have," I say.

"Well, your tooth brush is dry," she answers triumphantly. (You imagine anyone going and rubbing your toothbrush between finger and thumb like that—a practice surely wholly unhygienic.)

It got in the end so that if I wasn't going to clean my teeth I used to *wet the toothbrush* so as to be on the safe side; and although I do in fact clean my teeth twice a day, my toothbrush is always as wet as the toothbrush of a man who cleans his teeth every half hour or so. Incidentally, I never knew whether to praise or blame Mr. Midshipman Easy for using a second-hand toothbrush. There are very few toothbrushes in English fiction. I was surprised when I first read *Midshipman Easy* to discover that they had been invented in his day. I had thought they came in in my youth with washing-behind-your-ears and other modern practices.

My mother used to clean her teeth with salt, or with soot. I never failed to be impressed when she pushed her toothbrush up the chimney and proceeded to produce gleaming white teeth by the application of that blackcoated instrument. But then my mother's is a very resourceful family. Witness one of her brothers, who cured himself of baldness when well over eighty by rubbing his scalp with paraffin oil and a lump of concrete.[1]

I see I have headed this chapter "General Character and Disgusting Habits" but it is in fact only about my disgusting habits.

This gives a very fair indication of my general character.

[1] I am wrong here, they tell me. He used the lump of concrete for filing his finger nails. It was a very large lump deposited in his garden by the explosion of a bomb across the street.

Me as Dramatic Critic

Although I had to give way when they wouldn't let me call this book *Hopkins, the Man and His Work*, I am determined that His Work shall at least figure in a chapter or so, but to avoid overloading these pages with sonnets I will deal with some lesser aspects of my career.

James Agate once put his hand on my knee in a taxi, and Alan Dent once reviewed one of my books (adversely) in the *Observer*, otherwise my contact with the world of dramatic criticism has been confined to a long-standing friendship with J. C. Trewin and some singularly stimulating passages with St. John Ervine, including a walk with him at midnight through the crescents and squares of Bath while he discoursed about Irving, Horace Horsnell and other fine matters, J. C. Trewin concurring.

Then there were the two times I wrote dramatic notices for the *Spectator*. I did four pieces, really, but the third was a mere twelve lines about a play produced in the provincial city of Chichester, birthplace of William Collins, but no seat of the modern drama; and the fourth never appeared in print.

I ought perhaps to explain that my experience of the theatre before becoming dramatic critic for *The Spectator* consisted in occasional visits to pantomime, entertainments in Church Halls and the like, and the time I saw Max Miller at the Holborn Empire. All the same, I suppose for so brief a space as critic this provided sufficient background, and pantomime, after all, comprehends within itself almost every aspect of the drama. We choir boys used to go every year to the pantomime as a Christmas treat, accompanied by a curate or two, Mr. Chandler, the choirmaster, and Mr. Webber. For this outing we went to the old Theatre Royal at Bournemouth; I daresay the Hippodrome pantomime at Boscombe was considered too robust for young lads. Of several such visits (after all, despite an indifferent voice and my tendency to go on singing after the others had stopped, I was in the choir five or six years) I can recall only the most tenuous memories. In one pantomime a lady with a gentleman's cap on backwards sang a song beginning, "My old man's a dustman, what do you think of that? He wears a dustman's trousers and he wears a dustman's hat." When my old woman's old man was a dustman he wore no hat at all, see Chapter 23.

Another song was "An Egg and some Ham and an Onion".

We used to have chocolates, too, but I cannot remember whether we had a box each, or if they were only passed round. My mother had taught me such super politeness as a child that in the latter event I probably got nothing, from my nervous and highly involuntary habit of saying, "No, thank you," very firmly whenever anything nice was offered. A habit I have since lost.

But before those choir-treat pantomimes I had theatre experience dating back, I suppose, to the age of three or four. When my father was at the wars my mother used once a week to go to the Hip. with Aunt Ada. This was the Boscombe Hippodrome, happily still functioning, and the gods then cost fourpence. I suppose my sister and I got in for less. I had very little idea what was going on, but even at that early age I rejoiced when the stage was peopled with ladies. The only other distinct recollection I have is of a gentleman appearing out of a gas-oven with a blinding flash. He had black waxed whiskers and white teeth and brilliant angry eyes. What a way to earn a living!

The Boscombe Hippodrome, I think, is not to be confused with the Boscombe Theatre, for which a number of indifferent verse plays were issued in the mid-nineteenth century by the local bookseller and printer, Sidney Mate. (Some of this I am making up.) Neither is it to be confused with the private theatre of Sir Percy Shelley at Boscombe Manor, close by, which last time I saw it had some sort of horrible machinery in it to serve a night school; which shows how much the town of Bournemouth cares for its literary associations.

But it must not be supposed that my early grounding was wholly in the frivolous art of the music hall. I saw *The Importance of Being Earnest* when I was barely in my teens, and played in a drama of my own composing at a scout camp as early as 1929. What a piece of work that was, my first acted play! The hero (me) was O. Sniggerby Whelp, the great detective, and his prey none other than the Sneezer. Inspector Bullfrog (John French) was the third character, which made it two to one on the law. But the Sneezer was no ordinary criminal (I forget who played him.)

There were very few words in this drama, which required whole field for stage since the characters spent much time chasing one another. When it came to be acted the few words became still fewer, because John French forgot his. I remember rushing past him hissing, "Speak, you fool!"

It was at the same camp that I wrote the words for a patrol song for the Owls, and Arthur Searle wrote the music. The Owls had always been called the Lions, but that year word had gone forth from Baden-Powell that patrols ought to be called after native animals wherever possible, so we changed our name to Owls.

I could never get the rest of the patrol to learn the words and although the song was sung once, I think, at a camp fire, it was never sung again. Of course, I had no authority: I wasn't even a Second-class Scout and the patrol leader was a little boy only half my size, covered from head to foot with Badges.

As for Arthur Searle's music, I don't think that ever got beyond being hummed in mistake for a popular song which it somewhat resembled.

I was never a composer myself except that I liked at one time ruling five lines on a bit of paper and filling in fearsome patterns of notes with (ff) pretty often and occasionally (dim.) On one occasion (before I knew he couldn't read a note of music and only played by ear) I got Mr. Webber to try one of these pieces on the organ. I suppose the result wasn't encouraging to one who played by ear, for he never broached the matter again.

However, I must return to dramatic criticism, for after all I have never yet been entrusted with a notice of even a Wigmore Hall concert.

I'm not sure how far a dramatic critic should have been a practising playwright. Four or five of my works have been staged with varying success, including *Utterpug* aforementioned. And *Neptune Triumphant* was in a way a sort of opera; and (I am convinced) pretty average good. At least up to the standard of J. R. Planche, and *his* dramatic works fill five sizeable volumes. They are fairly frequently met with on the second-hand trays, and hardly ever bought.

All I remember about *The Laureate*—if that was what it was called—is that when I had answered the cry of "Author! Author!" someone told me afterwards that I need not have gone on bowing so long. I thought you had to go on until they stopped clapping, and it appeared that they didn't care to stop clapping while I was still bowing. A very difficult situation.

.All this, apart from my appearances in plays by others (let me see, I was in *Ask Beckles*, and *The Sport of Kings*, and *A Night at an Inn*—well, everybody has been in *A Night at an Inn*, but not everybody has been the bloodchilling shriek at the end—and even quite classical stuff like *A Hundred Years Old*) made excellent background experience for *The Spectator*. So when Derek Hudson rang up and said their chap was ill, or something, and could I do the Marx Brothers, I said yes.

And now I will do as James Agate used to do: I will reprint a bit. But as this notice is quite short, I will reprint it all. I find (then) that I wrote thus of the Marx Brothers:

Two Musketeers? Two Blind Mice? It would be perfectly possible, yet even as we concede the possibility we are conscious that there lacketh something still. "We take no note of Time," the poet Young remarks, "but from its loss." Can this be true also of Groucho? Certainly I was never able to take in quite all that Harpo and Chico were up to, because every time a gentleman in the audience joined in with a particularly distinctive laugh (and there were several such gentlemen in the audience) I thought nervously that here was the missing link and that incredible moustache was about to swim before me. So as I write it is only about the absent Groucho that I have any illusions. Harpo and Chico I have seen in the flesh, and now in retrospect they appear a little less than life size. Accomplished, loveable, funny, all these—they turn out to be human after all.

Harpo looks like an excellent copy of himself by a minor master in the same school, but the things he is given to do are unworthy of him. Once only, for a few minutes, is this magnificent mime, sitting mute and adoring at the feet of a lovely singer, allowed to move us with pity and love by the perfect set of an eyebrow and the droop of an under-lip. Most of the rest of the time he is popping on and off the stage without useful purpose. It is no encouragement to a great comic to give him a pair of cardboard pantomime scissors three feet long to run after the girls with. Chico, possibly a lesser artist than his brother, is in the present show the more convincing. His voice endears him at once to everybody, for what he says and how he says it. His timing and rhythm are perfect. He is the sort of person one wants to go and shake hands with; he reinforces our opinion that there must be good some-where in the world.

If anybody says I didn't write that because it is signed "Christopher Adams" in the original, let me tell him that Adams was my mother's maiden name, and Christopher is after St. Christopher's Buildings where we had the one-room flat after we were first married. Everything is done for a reason: take St. John, our black cat, for example: he's nothing to do with the Church. We called him after St. John Ervine, so eloquent on Irving, in the midnight streets of Bath.

Illustrated by the Author

"Of Hartley's hypothetical vibrations in his hypothetical oscillating ether of the nerves, which is the first and most obvious distinction between his system and that of Aristotle, I shall say little," Coleridge tells us. In my opinion, he was very wise. "Enough, or Too Much," says Blake. It is important to know when to stop. Accordingly, I shall not reprint my criticism of *Kiss Me, Kate*.

I must indeed hasten on to another matter that has been troubling my thought as this book draws towards a close. *What about the illustrations?* Augustus Hare's autobiography was illustrated, and so ought mine to be, especially as, now I come to think of it, my moustache although less luxuriant than his, has the same dying fall. I am not handsome, but you would know me again.

If photographs will serve, that side of the matter can be taken care of. There are many photographs of me, including the one wearing Hugh Miller's hat which he sold (or more probably, gave) to me the day I had my first London haircut.

That was a day! When I had been living over Charlie Lahr's bookshop for about five weeks he said to me one morning that one of his customers who had a haircutting establishment off Charing Cross Road had volunteered to cut my hair for nothing. I suppose it was for the advertisement. A day for this barbering marathon was appointed and I went along, furnished with minute directions. These were very necessary because there are a number of haircutting shops in the Charing Cross Road area, and attendance at the wrong one would have been embarrassing, for I had no money. Perhaps Charles had borrowed my last sixpence.

And when I got back, sufficiently shorn, Hugh Miller gave me his hat. (MILLER, Hugh, 1802–1856, author of *The Old Red Sandstone* and other works, he was not the Miller mentioned above.)

I used to wear this hat most of the time, for I'd never really had a hat of my own after Douglas's wolf-cub cap wore out. Of course, there was my mortar board still somewhere at home, but even in Red Lion Street a mortar board would have been thought eccentric without an Eton suit.

And finally I had myself photographed in the thing. In those days you could get three picture-postcard photographs for a shilling, and in a flush moment I had a shillingsworth: of which four-pennyworth survives. They were slightly smaller than regular picture postcards, and I thought this rather in the nature of sharp practice. If you advertise a thing by a familiar but vague label like "postcard" you ought to supply what people understand by the term.

Anyhow, I gave one of the photographs, I think, to Margaret. One I sent home. And the third, which is the surviving one, I sent to my ancient ally J. C. Powys *to look at and return*; both these things he very promptly did.

Then there's the picture of me sitting in a Brussels café with a glass in front of me and an expression of cynical despair on my face. Both arms are slightly forward, enabling the single stripe to be seen and no error. One of the first things even a junior N.C.O. learns is never to be photographed with his arms behind his back. Warrant Officers, who wear badges of rank on the wrist, often have to assume theatrical poses, or else try to look as if they were taken unawares while scratching the nose.

I suppose a suitable frontispiece would be that painting of me by Mariella, although it would have to be explained that since then I have put on a little weight, and to bring the thing into line it would be necessary to ink a moustache in.

But none of these things fits the phrase, "Illustrated by the Author." Augustus Hare had lots of little line drawings of

churches in Italy and things like that. I think I have one or two
trifles of water-colour which would serve.

When I was about eight I discovered a talent (since lost) for
drawing ships. With this went a wide knowledge of the names
of ships, the steamship companies that owned them, and even
the ports to which they sailed, though unlike my friend H. M.
Tomlinson I didn't grow up to sail to such ports myself. Tommy
had bowsprits at the bottom of the garden, but nothing came in
to Bournemouth Pier but the *Empress of India*, *Monarch* and
Victoria (Messrs. Cosens & Co's buff-funnel Steamers, as the
bills called them) and the *Balmoral*, *Lorna Doone* and *Bournemouth
Queen* (Southampton, Isle of Wight and South of England
Steam Packet Co.—white funnels with black tops.) I never
attempted to draw these local vessels; they were not big
enough, and in addition the perspective of paddles is the very
devil.

But I was particularly good with the *Mauretania* sailing either
way, from left to right or from right to left; even, marvellously
foreshortened, coming right at you out of the paper. Looking
back, I'm inclined to think my virtuosity with the *Mauretania* in
this position almost equalled that of Blake with his "Ancient of
Days"—though admittedly Blake had the advantage of colour.

I can't quite see, however, how a drawing of the *Mauretania*
would serve to illustrate my autobiography. I never sailed in
her, nor even saw her close up, though at the age of four or
thereabouts I saw the *Berengaria* from Netley beach. Cousin
Phyllis on that occasion mocked two supercilious bystanders,
one of whom said, "The *Imperator's* just gone out," with the
ready rhyming shaft, "The *Havatomata's* just gone out." I
suppose that large, rather Teutonic-looking liner had just been
handed over to Britain.

Of course, the *Mauretania* of my youth was the famous record
breaker, with four funnels. I never drew two-funnelled ships,
except one of the White Star liners, the *Homeric*, which I rather
liked because she was the largest twin-screw vessel in the
world (34,000 tons.)

I suppose we could have a drawing of the *Mauretania* if it were accompanied by a legend explaining that in his youth the author was much influenced by the information that if one of her funnels (it didn't say which one) were placed on its side you could drive a tram through it. But I'm not sure that that wasn't the *Majestic*, John French's favourite ship. (56,000 tons—but I write from memory. Incidentally I never believed that the *Leviathan* was 59,000 tons. It was a system of measurement, I used to explain, not countenanced by Lloyds and invented by the Americans so that they could have the biggest ship in the world. By *our* standards she was only 54,000 tons. This was a great comfort to John French.)

So much for the *Mauretania*, which when she was not sailing the ocean was lying down engulphing trams, or uprearing herself against St. Paul's Cathedral to prove herself longer than the dome is tall and—on a famous occasion—meeting the *Flying Dutchman* going the other way.

My most powerful personal memory of great ships at this time is the impression made on me by seeing hundreds of teapots hanging on hooks along the ceiling of a Union Castle liner's kitchen. But I believe this negligible vessel had only one funnel. We visited her in Southampton Docks, on one of the occasions when we were spending a holiday there, at Mrs. Hardy's in Bugle Street. I once read years after how many teapots they have to have.

But, even if suitable, none of these ship drawings survive. My drawing of the Mill, Sully, however, framed and glazed, is readily available. It hangs in the back kitchen now, but it has hung in the front hall in its day.

It was at the Mill, Sully, that for the only time in my career I put a man on a charge. The man didn't think lance-corporals had the power to do this, and I wasn't sure myself, but I put a bold (and very red) face on it. What was his name, I wonder? I well remember his offence. We were in an orchard, and he was throwing apples at the cooks. We had just arrived and they were struggling to erect a cookhouse and get some tea—

and I wanted my tea—and all this chap could do was throw apples.

So I put him on a charge. Having done this I sought out Staff Sergeant P. and explained the whole affair, and that was the last I ever heard of it. I suppose in a way the chap is still under open arrest.

I doubt if the Mill, Sully, was ever quite the same again after we left it. So my drawing has real historical value: "The Mill as it was. From the drawing by Hopkins, dated '44. *Louvre*."

One hot July afternoon I made my drawing. It is about eleven by nine and is on stiff brown paper—the cover of an Army Form A.3091 (foolscap). It is executed in an interesting medium, not commonly used by artists: i.e., part pencil, part coloured chalk, part wax crayon, and part green ink borrowed from Corporal Naylor. The perspective is interesting. It owes something to my early studies of the *Mauretania*, but almost nothing to William Blake.

Another work of this period is my drawing of Bayeux Cathedral, made (as no doubt many others have been, and photographs too, I expect) from half-way down a narrow street leading up at an angle to the west front. I suppose it was the angle that did it; at all events, the great edifice appears to be in grave danger of collapse and if that happened the whole of the little street going up at an angle would be obliterated. So perhaps it's just as well I have preserved my drawing.

After the war I did those strange grotesque coloured drawings that Beresford Egan spoke so highly of; but he didn't ask me to give him one, and I always think that is the test.

So, taking all into account, I don't think this book had better be "illustrated by the author". And it is a phrase which I always look upon with disfavour—Augustus Hare notwithstanding. Either the author can draw and he can't write, or he can write and he can't draw. What about Robert Gibbings, then? it may be asked. But to this I have no answer, and I pass on.

Collectors, Beware

Although I have always wanted to be recognised as a "writer chap"—the phrase is from John Symonds—my ambitions have ever been of the modest sort. A couple of fairly successful books a year, and the occasional article in a magazine would suit me very well. I have no permanent lust to be pointed out in the street with the excited cry, "There goes Hopkins!" although in those early London days I so much enjoyed knowing I was Hopkins when everyone else was kept in the dark about it. I have no great desire to give my autograph, and indeed a whole host of little boys in Rouen who asked for it received the bold inscription, "B. L. Montgomery, F. M." in lieu. The thought of sitting in a department store writing my name in copies of this book before milling crowds appals me, though I could do with the money.

But I have always wanted to figure in the catalogues of second-hand book sellers, and this desire is wholly altruistic, for by the time a book is sold second-hand the author's chance of profit is gone for ever. But to be "collected" is the real accolade. Many writers who sell their books by the hundred thousand are never collected in the strict sense; and others of whom the general reading public never hears, yet command high prices in the catalogues. At present I am in a third category: I have never been generally heard of, and I am left alone by the collectors. Probably the only certain way to get into the second-hand catalogues is to open a second-hand bookshop oneself and issue one's own. Just as when nobody else would publish my poems I invented the Grasshopper Press to do it for me and lost quite a mort of money; but I still have most of the books.

Well, as recorded above, I have now and then figured among the authors of the sought-after first editions, and not long after I became reconciled to that mediority in authorship which is the lot of most writers I received a request from a celebrated London bookseller for a "check-list" of my works. Now this gentleman deals in "modern first editions" and the purpose of a check-list is to enable him to deal expeditiously and accurately with inquiries from two Americans who collect my writings in the mistaken belief that I am another Hopkins. So when they cry, what was his first book, my bookseller friend can at once confidently answer, *Twelve Poems* (1937). Of course that was long before the days of the Grasshopper Press. *Twelve Poems* was printed in Charminster Road, Bournemouth, one Saturday afternoon.

A. E. Page the printer and I laboured valiantly at those twelve poems, I remember; I in writing them to the best of my ability, and he in setting them in Goudy Old Face, ten-point, or it may have been Times Roman. We printed ninety-nine copies, he turning the handle of the press and I (the professional author) hovering about with an expression of eager disinterest. Twenty-five copies were signed by the author, and of these two were signed also by John Cowper Powys who contributed a slight foreword (it was a sentence out of a letter). I mention this in order to get catalogued under Powys, J. C.—see Hopkins, K., when the time comes. And to give the Powys collectors something else to burrow and scratch for !

Twelve Poems (the best bibliographical dictionaries will tell you) is not in the British Museum. They are wrong. I must be looked up in the catalogue of that great library not under HOPKINS (Kenneth) but under HOPKINS (Hector Kenneth). I have never discovered how they got on to the Hector part, but I suspect it was that anthology I hastened to publish in Brussels when I was there with the Mobile Laundry.

It was a wild scramble in 1945 in Brussels to get books published though a lot of us did—of course it was easier for the officers. But who ever heard of a lance-corporal who had written a book? All the same, I got this anthology published with a choice quotation from Dryden on the title page—the reader will mark my fondness for Dryden: the present book carries him on the title, too. Well, also on the title page of *The English Lyric* my name appeared (a size larger than Dryden's) as "Kenneth Hopkins", but under the frontispiece for some reason they put "H. K. Hopkins". Oh, it was me all right— we couldn't get Dryden in time—and the likeness is faithful enough, but that extra "H" must have caused a good deal of coming and going at the British Museum, for I notice that against one entry the "H" has been inked in before the Kenneth, and then of course the rot began. A bit later, in another hand, the "ector" has been added, and the whole formidable third-of-a-column taken out from between HOPKINS (Keith) and HOPKINS (Kurt) and set back raggedly among the Hopkinses (H.) (Howard) and even (Hetty).

But that came later. I was telling you about *Twelve Poems*. This work has the interesting distinction of being bound in wallpaper and a "tall copy" (as we bibliographers say) may be as much as eight inches high. The tallest copy I ever handled was about eight inches high at the front and hardly more than six at the back. The scissors slipped.

Most writers, even the ones who eventually get to be famous, begin with poetry of a sort. But I have a distinction which is much rarer. My first book had sixteen pages; my second had only eight (not counting the covers, which again were wallpaper: it came, I expect, from Holts). As for *New Sonnets* (1938) that had a mere six pages and only contained four sonnets.

So far as I can remember at this remote distance the second book (which was called, rather grandly, I thought, *Recent Poetry*) had only eight pages not because my output had slackened, but because this was found to come cheaper. The profit on the first transaction, some fifteen shillings, was ploughed back into the business to become *Recent Poetry*. Because only thirty-three copies were printed this is now one of the rarer of the early works and I think as much as two shillings might reasonably be asked for a copy; and indeed I would give something like that myself, for I have only one and it is desirable to have at least two copies of one's own works, one in the original binding and one suitably bound in morocco to stand on the mantlepiece.

Of course, as we know, I'm not only a poet. When I got back from the war I went into the best-seller market with great success and if there had been any money in it I'd have been there to this day. I don't mind admitting that about this time one of my works was serialised in *Home Notes* and I can prove it. Of course, it was under another name, but that was nothing to me. I have written with varying success under sixteen *noms-de-plume* in my time, and two pseudonyms.

By the way, people seldom publish poems under a *nom-de-plume*. Poets are a conceited lot, and always think they are good; so they carefully put their own name to it usually. I remember when I was seventeen tearing down through the busiest of the traffic at Bournemouth on my bicycle with a girl called Sylvia on the back. Over my shoulder as we rushed round the perilous bends I was discussing the merits of my verse. "Oh, well, if you think you're good, that's the main thing," she conceded. I wondered afterwards if poetry really interested her.

The check list of my works makes impressive reading to anyone who has not examined the volumes under review. There are twenty-nine items (counting two that aren't out yet) and *Spring in Park Lane* sold well over 120,000. That was one of the prose works; and of course the illustrations helped. Few of my collections of verse have reached a sale of three figures.

The rarest of my works, and one few collectors can hope to acquire is *Bridal Song for Helen* (1949). This is a six-line poem in a four-page folder (4 pp. is the trade term) of which twelve copies were printed. I say twelve, but there may be one or two "spoils" still lingering in the printer's workshop, for these chaps, some of them, seldom sweep up. I gave two or three copies to Helen, together with a handsome wedding gift (a book) and two or three I issued to the more indefatigible Hopkins collectors. Somewhere I retain the remainder, waiting for the price to rise. It was found impracticable to bind one in morocco so I stuck it in something else, where it makes the cover bulge slightly.

I ought in fairness to explain that, generally speaking, the demand for my writings among collectors of "modern first editions" is so inconsiderable that my bookseller friend's request for a check list was hardly justified. What he really asked for in the first place was a check list of the works of an eminent writer, lately deceased, of whose works he knew I had a complete set. But, as a polite afterthought, he added that a check list of my own valuable writings would be a great boon. I took no umbrage at being a mere footnote to the main requirement. I was, indeed, foolish enough to be flattered. But I did take a mild revenge.

I furnished my check list by return of post; but he is still waiting for a tale of the works of that eminent writer lately deceased.

Recent Credentials

There is a phrase in one of Belloc's novels—probably in *Mr. Petre*—that has kept in my mind for twenty years and more, ever since the days when I swallowed almost the entire works of Belloc whole (and a man might do much worse). A character is being conducted to the office of the manager of a great bank, and he passes engravings of successive head offices of the concern which—says Belloc—served to mark a progressive deterioration in the architectural sense of bankers. The lesson can be applied in many departments besides architecture.

That is why these later pages have contained few specimens of my verses. Suppose—the thought comes—the later work is thought on the whole no striking advance on the things quoted from the parish magazine of thirty years ago. But it wasn't that sort of corrupion the poet in my book was meant to suffer from. I only intended by that convenient quotation to suggest that the innocence of youth had been replaced by the wariness of age; and indeed it was to make this interpretation clear that I avoided bringing in too many girls, although I recollect now that I once knew a girl named Thora. There ought certainly to be a wistful reference to her, but the fact is, her name apart, I haven't the remotest notion about her—colour of eyes, street she lived in, dress she wore, all are forgotten. Thora or Flora, was she?

But one must after all keep some sort of faith with one's Muse. There are few enough markets for poems and the chance to introduce them into one's books cannot be ignored. I put four of my poems into *The English Lyric*, and as that anthology was supposed to represent the best short poems from the earliest times to the death of Tennyson I had the grace to mark my four "Anon." By the same device I have got rid of one or two other trifles elsewhere, but there is neither fame nor fortune in it. And if ever I reprint those fugitive pieces in a book boldly marked "by Kenneth Hopkins" all sorts of people are going to start up and say, "That one is fifteenth-century Anon," or "That one was published by Peter Lodge years ago." Alas, *I* am Peter Lodge, and Paul Marsh, and John Butler, and the rest of the sixteen . . .

I have said that the Saturdays inclined me to writing shorter and shorter poems. They also set me to writing light verse, which I hadn't tackled much before: for a young poet of genius isn't likely to waste time on any theme below high tragedy, the death of love, the transitoriness of youth, etc., except occasionally to glance at a flank or a thigh. Please don't think this statement dogmatic: it is based on close personal observation! Well——

I discovered that there is a good deal of fun to be had from writing a poem on another poet's theme. I have dozens of books of minor Victorian verse, and I used to go through these and pick titles that appealed to me and see if I could do anything better than the original poet had managed. Like this:

LINES

Suggested by the poem, "Farewell to the E. & A. Co's
S.S. 'European' " by Wm. Igglesden, Commander in Her
Majesty's Indian Navy.

Float on, thou fairest ship was ever seen,
The E. & A. Co's S.S. 'European'!
And to the distant shores of England take
Your path o'er trackless wave, and no mistake.

What ship, two-funnelled, masted-thrice, is that?
It is the 'European' on her way.
The air is balmy and the sea is flat.
She should have been at Dover yesterday.

"I think that something ails this mighty ship,"
Says Captain Spinley, pulling at his lip;
Just then with sharp report the boilers burst,
'Mid gentlemanly cries of "Women and Children first."

Down plunges prow, up rises stern behind,
  Her bilges have been pierced with disaster;
In local press lugubrious tidings find:
  "Lost: 'European'; William Spinley, Master."

Anyone who possesses Igglesden's *Poetical Miscellanea* (1858) may decide for himself to whom the palm should go. I will only add that for this type of composition a rich badness is necessary and that can only be attained by an almost complete lack of humour in the writer. Other titles (one from Parnell, who was a much more considerable poet than most of those consulted for this purpose) upon which I attempted poems were "On Hearing that J. W. Croker, Esq., Secretary to the Admiralty had fallen from his Horse" (by John Taylor), "An Epistle from Alexias, a noble Roman, to his wife, whom he left on his Wedding-day, with a design to visit the Eastern churches" (by Elizabeth Rowe), "On Bishop Burnet's being set on Fire in his Closet" (Parnell), and from Landor, "To a Green Lizard Called Ramorino."

Landor's poem I approached in no spirit of mockery; it was the lizard's name that appealed to me.

TO A GREEN LIZARD CALLED RAMORINO

How many seasons since the leaning sun
Across those patterned scales let fall his ray
As on the burning brick, unmoving, unwinking, lay
The lizard Ramorino, lazily alive!

Landor a hundred years since saw him run
Along the lichened wall and disappear
With sudden twist and swift precipitate dive
Into some cranny secret and secure.

None may know Ramorino any more
Though but a monent since he seemed just here
With darting tongue and apprehensive eye
Upon this same sun-hot and mottled wall
Watching the sun bend through the slanting sky.

Whatever is lovely, even the green lizard, all
Bright things, seen or unseen, somewhere, these—
Colour and grace and movement—have their surcease.

Another fruitful source of ideas is a classical dictionary. I have an old copy of Lempriére, and I got into the habit of turning the pages until a name took my fancy, and then trying to condense the paragraph into four lines: good or bad, these four contain more pregnant information than many novels:

THEMISTO

Hypseus' daughter she, of four sons mother,
Third wife of Thebes' sovereign, Athamas;
Seeking to slay his children by another,
By sad mischance her own she slew, alas.

Poor Themisto! I have often wondered what happened next.

Yet another way of getting your thinking partly done for you is to consult the *Annual Register*. I chance to have a run of the first sixty or seventy volumes of this, and they are a fine source of inspiration if you happen to be interested in rape, murder, arson, and various sorts of sudden death. The proper method here is to give a brief synopsis of the matter under notice and then launch straight off into your poem. So:

Dec. 2, 1823. Died . . . In consequence of a wound received the preceding day, while shooting in his plantations, by a gun going off as he was getting through a hedge, and lodging its contents in his right side—Robert Viner, Esq., of Eathorp.

O fatal morning of December 2,
When Robert Viner saunters into view,
The loaded gun upon his shoulder set
That never turned on Robert Viner yet;

What thorny hedge impedes his progress strait
Nor yet affords a gap or five-barr'd gate?
Impatient Viner battles with the shrub,
Disdainful of a vegetable snub;

But gun on shoulder catches on a twig,
Gives Robert Viner shrewd and hurtful dig,
Discharging load of pellets in his side—
And thus it was that Robert Viner died.

If it is thought that even after well over a century it is unkind to write thus lightly of a matter which must have been of great moment to those concerned, I will not defend myself, but will pass on to a last class of light verse which is entirely fictitious, and isn't even written by the aid of bits out of books. This is the epitaph which appears on the surface to be funny—or at least is intended so—but on reflection is found to be profoundly tragic. Like this:

EPITAPH

On an Old Woman, eaten by mistake
by the Portman Hounds.

She walks along the lane collecting twigs
To kindle her poor fire; a distant bay
Gives notice that the Hounds will pass this way,
But that is nothing new to Jenny Spriggs;
They come: the Leader pauses, takes a bite,
Finds Jenny's elderly, but tastes all right,
Falls to, the others with him: to be short,
They eat her, not in anger but for sport;
The twigs they leave upon the wayside stones,
But bury, as dogs will, the bloody bones.
She, being old, has neither hope nor friend,
Yet Jenny Spriggs deems this a dreadful end.

Really, I have seldom read or written a more unpleasant poem. And now, since I have unintentionally embarked upon a little anthology of specimens, I will give one or two examples of short pieces imitated from the masters—Herrick, for example:

MODESTY LIVES IN FAMILIARITY

After twelve yeares when her I naked see
Jenny with blush turns her bare front to me,
From which has fallen shift and shadow sheere
As darks must from the Sunne all disappeare.

TO JENNY, ON HER BEDDE

My brown girl lies along the linnen sheete
Cleane as a catt and as the catt is, neat;
Pure as bees' honey, Jenny my wife, and sweet:
I'll kisse her all, beginning with a teate.

Or Blake:

> Love moves beyond the reach of spoiling hands
> And leads into the room where Jesus stands.

Blake again:

> What beauty is so occupied my thought
> I saw not all Heaven's light in a dew-drop caught.

And, finally, since throughout this book there has been much talk of sonnets, a poem in fourteen lines:

LOVE AT NINETEEN

She'd be a wonder naked! O she'd be rare
To hold in strong arms gently, burnished and bare
With parted lips, closed eyes and loosened hair!
Her body's bounds enclose in single space
Every delight that in love's need has place—
Love looks on love in her small flawless face
For she is made so intricately fair
All must find all they look for mirrored there.

She's a new world to open and explore:
How firm, warmth, smooth, her naked shoulders, thighs,
Under the trembling, questing hand that lies
Along her body, the kiss that seals her eyes!
O, catch her up, quick with the promise of more
Uncharted deeps, unmapped discoveries!

Rising Forty

And now: where do we go from here?—as Greville Poke used to say at Editorial Conferences when he was with us at *Everybody's*. I have told, in some sort, the tale of my days from birth to thirty-five, the traditional half-way point. Looking over these pages, I have detected a good many omissions, but I have determined not to go back and put things in; for the habit of autobiography, once acquired, is not easily discouraged, and I shall certainly want to write about myself again. Indeed, I am reluctant to stop now, but the book has reached a suitable length.

And where do I go from here?

I can remain in Fleet Street, with its constant shifting of men and loyalties, its fascination, its excitements and tensions and dramas. It is a very parochial place, too. In Fleet Street you can be a person of consequence one day, and stabbed in the back the next—as you can in most walks of life, except that elsewhere you are less likely to be assailed at the same time with hypocrisy, malice, and all uncharitableness.

Or I can decide, as many have done before me, that journalism is a fine profession to have been in, after you are out of it; but not the job for a life-time. "You have one life, one little life . . ." Spend it in Fleet Street and be damned!

Well, I don't know; and I suppose I shan't know until it is time to write the next chapter of my life story. Few of us do the things we intended, or achieve the things we have hoped for. I have at least been lucky in achieving things I didn't venture to hope for—a generous measure of happiness, some experiences of love that I didn't put into my poems, many good friends and a

235

few sufficient enemies, and all kinds of jolly auxiliary benefits not separately noted here.

The corruption of a poet is the generation of a critic . . . and I have learned this much in forty years: to be alive at all is an unlooked for chance, to be alive and happy is a wonder. Yet— and this is the real miracle—happiness is neither costly nor rare. Millions have it always at their elbow, as I have.